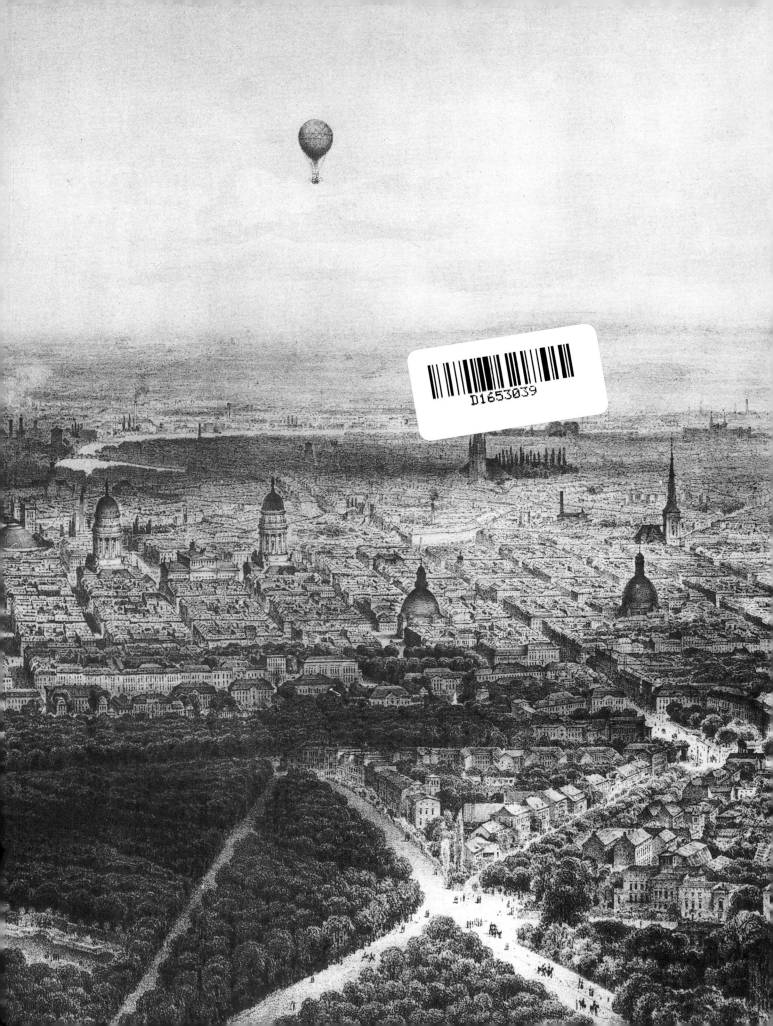

Rainer Laabs
Das Brandenburger Tor

Rainer Laabs

Das Brandenburger Tor

Brennpunkt deutscher Geschichte
Focus of German History

Deutsch/English

Ullstein

© 1990 by Verlag Ullstein GmbH, Frankfurt/M. – Berlin
Redaktion/Redaction: Christian Seeger
Übersetzung ins Englische/Translation into English:
Hild Wollenhaupt
Typographie und Layout/Typography and Layout: Dieter Speck
Alle Rechte vorbehalten/All rights reserved
Reproduktionen/Reproductions: Haußmann Reprotechnik, Darmstadt
Satz/Typeset: Utesch Satztechnik GmbH, Hamburg
Druck und Bindung/Printed and bound: Grafica Editoriale, Bologna
Printed in Italy 1990
ISBN 3 550 07404 2

CIP-Titelaufnahme der Deutschen Bibliothek

Laabs, Rainer:
Das Brandenburger Tor: Brennpunkt deutscher Geschichte;
deutsch/englisch / Rainer Laabs. [Übers. ins Engl.: Hild
Wollenhaupt]. – Berlin: Ullstein, 1990
ISBN 3-550-07404-2

Für Katharina, Friederike und Ullrich

Inhalt/Contents

9 Vorwort
10 »Das Stadt-Thor von Athen zum Modelle genommen«
13 Die Quadriga
16 Napoleon, der Pferdedieb
18 Berliner Biedermeier
20 Drei Kriege
23 Vierzig Jahre Frieden
25 Fehlstart einer Republik
27 »Im lodernden Schein der Fackeln«
29 Kalter Krieg
33 Die Mauer
35 »Wir sind ein Volk!«

39 Preface
40 »Taking the Athens Town-Gate for Model«
43 The Quadriga
45 Napoleon, the Horse Thief
47 Berlin »Biedermeier«
49 Three Wars
52 Forty Years of Peace
54 False Start of a Republic
56 »By the Light of Flaming Torches«
58 Cold War
62 The Wall
64 »We Are One People!«

65 Bildteil / Illustrations
206 Danksagung / Acknowledgements
206 Ausgewählte Literatur / Selected Bibliography
208 Bildnachweis / Illustration Credits

Vorwort

Zwei Daten haben bei diesem Buch Pate gestanden: Der 6. August 1991 und der 22. Dezember 1989. Das erste Datum zeigt den 200. Jahrestag der Fertigstellung des Brandenburger Tores an – es steht für die bewegte Geschichte dieses Bauwerks. Das zweite Datum markiert die Wiedereröffnung des Tores nach achtundzwanzigjähriger Sperrung durch die Berliner Mauer – es steht für die Symbolik des Langhans-Baus.

In den zwei Jahrhunderten seiner Existenz stand das Brandenburger Tor weit häufiger im Brennpunkt der deutschen Geschichte als jedes andere Bauwerk Deutschlands. Vom Einzug Napoleons 1806 über die Siegesparaden der Bismarckschen Einigungskriege, die Novemberrevolution 1918, Hitlers »Machtergreifung« am 30. Januar 1933, die Kapitulation am 8. Mai 1945, den Volksaufstand in der DDR am 17. Juni 1953, den Mauerbau am 13. August 1961 bis hin zum Zusammenbruch des DDR-Regimes am 9. November 1989: Stets war das Tor Schauplatz oder Kulisse für großartige Feiern, Aufmärsche und Kundgebungen oder aber für Manifestationen politischen oder militärischen Scheiterns der Nation. Die vielen, oft dramatischen Ereignisse, die sich hinter den genannten Daten verbergen und deren Zeuge das Brandenburger Tor wurde, haben es zu einem einzigartigen Symbol der deutschen Geschichte gemacht.

Es gibt andere Bauwerke, die deutsche Geschichte symbolisieren, etwa das Aachener Münster, die Wartburg, die Frankfurter Paulskirche, der Kölner Dom oder auch das Reichstagsgebäude in Berlin. Sie alle aber stehen nur für bestimmte geschichtliche Etappen oder geistige Strömungen. Es gibt andere Monumente, die bewußt geschaffen wurden, um als nationales Symbol zu dienen, etwa das Leipziger Völkerschlachtdenkmal, das Hermannsdenkmal im Teutoburger Wald, die Walhalla, das Niederwalddenkmal oder das Kaiser-Wilhelm-Nationaldenkmal auf dem Kyffhäuser. Sie alle müssen sich heute mit der Rolle bloßer Sehenswürdigkeiten begnügen.

Gerade weil es nicht von vornherein als nationale Pilgerstätte konzipiert worden ist, gerade weil sich gleichermaßen Höhen und Tiefen deutscher Geschichte in ihm widerspiegeln, ist das Brandenburger Tor nationales Symbol geworden und als solches glaubwürdig und unumstritten. Wie es in diese Rolle hineingewachsen ist, soll der vorliegende Band dokumentieren.

»Das Stadt-Thor von Athen zum Modelle genommen«

Als man im Frühsommer 1788 daranging, das alte Brandenburger Tor, das die Berliner Dorotheenstadt westlich zum Tiergarten hin begrenzte, abzureißen, war es gerade vierundfünfzig Jahre alt. 1734 war es unter König Friedrich Wilhelm I. in einfachen barocken Formen errichtet worden. Wir kennen sein Aussehen durch eine Radierung aus dem Jahre 1764: zwei barocke Torpfosten, geschmückt mit Pilastern und Trophäen, die seitlichen Durchgänge mit Vasen verziert (1, 2*). Des Nachts war es mit Holztoren verschlossen, doch tagsüber entfaltete sich hier bereits ein recht lebhafter Verkehr von und nach Berlin.

Der Berliner Chronist Friedrich Nikolai gibt 1786 folgende Beschreibung von diesem Ort: »Am Brandenburger Thore, rechts nach der Spree zu, liegt der große Exerzierplatz. Diesseits desselben führt eine Allee, die Churfürstenallee genannt, nach einem großen Platze an der Spree ... Auf der Seite nach der Spree ist den ganzen Sommer durch eine Anzahl Zelte und Hütten aufgeschlagen, woselbst allerhand Erfrischungen verkauft werden ... An schönen Sommernachmittagen, sonderlich des Sonntags und Feyertags, gegen 6 Uhr pflegen hier einige tausend Spazierende zu Fuß, zu Pferde, und in Wagen zusammen zu kommen, wobey öfters, auf Befehl des Gouverneurs, die Musik der in Berlin in Garnison liegenden Infanterie- und Artillerie-Regiments in die anliegenden Büsche verteilt werden, welches zusammen ein sehr reizendes Schauspiel macht.«

Beiderseits des Tores gruppierten sich kleinere, schmucklose Gebäude. Von der Stadt aus gesehen links das Wachlokal und rechts ein Haus für den Steuerbeamten sowie das Spritzenhaus. Des weiteren seit 1767 rechts die Kaserne für das Herzog Friederichsche Infanterieregiment. Alles in allem keine häßliche Anlage. Und doch stieß sie auf Kritik. So heißt es in der Schrift »Kritische Anmerkungen über den Zustand der Baukunst in Berlin und Potsdam« aus dem Jahre 1776: »Besonders verdiente wohl das Brandenburger Thor, in Ansehung seiner vortrefflichen Lage, mehr Ansehen zu erhalten.«

König Friedrich Wilhelm II. von Preußen scheint derselben Ansicht gewesen zu sein. Und so war er es wohl, der den Auftrag zum Entwurf eines neuen Stadttores an Carl Gotthard Langhans vergab. Dieser legte seinem König prompt eine Denkschrift vor, in der es heißt: »Die Lage des Brandenburger-Thores ist in ihrer Art ohnstreitig die schönste von der ganzen Welt, um hiervon gehörig Vortheile zu ziehen, und dem Thore so viel Oefnung zu geben, als möglich ist, habe ich bey dem Bau des neuen Thores das Stadt-Thor von Athen zum Modelle genommen ...«

Wer war dieser Mann, der hier seinem König den Plan für eines der schönsten Bauwerke Berlins unterbreitete? Carl Gotthard Langhans wurde am 15. Dezember 1732 in Landeshut in Schlesien geboren. Er starb am 1. Oktober 1808 in Grüneiche bei Breslau. Während seines Architekturstudiums führten ihn Reisen nach Italien, Holland, England und Frankreich. Seit 1775 Oberbaurat, konzentrierte sich sein anfängliches Schaffen überwiegend auf seine Heimat Schlesien, bis er 1786 nach Berlin gerufen wurde, wo er später Direktor des Oberhofbauamtes werden sollte. Von Langhans stammen so bedeutende Bauten wie das Belvedere im Park des Schlosses Charlottenburg, das Marmorpalais in Potsdam, aber auch das im Sinne der Neugotik ergänzte Turmoberteil der Berliner Marienkirche. Als Innenarchitekt wirkte er in Schloß Rheinsberg, wo er das Treppenhaus und den Mu-

---

* Die in Klammern gesetzten Zahlen im Text verweisen auf die Abbildungen.

schelsaal schuf, sowie im Schloß Bellevue, dessen Festsaal er entwarf. Von seinen Theaterbauten ist besonders das erste deutsche Nationaltheater hervorzuheben, das auf dem Berliner Gendarmenmarkt stand und 1817 abbrannte. Doch heute ist der Name Langhans vor allem mit seinem Hauptwerk, dem Brandenburger Tor, verbunden.

Der Hinweis von Langhans in seinem Bericht an den König, daß er sich bei seinem Entwurf die Propyläen in Athen, also den Eingang zur Akropolis, zum Vorbild genommen habe, veranlaßte Johann Gottfried Schadow, in seinem Buch »Kunstwerke und Kunstansichten« wie folgt über seinen Kollegen zu spotten: »War es Mißtrauen gegenüber eigenen Ideen oder Bequemlichkeit, genug, er entlehnte gerne. Auf seinen Reisen hatte er seine Mappen gefüllt, und eine Wiederholung anerkannter Meisterwerke dünkte ihm sicherer als neue Originale von unser einem.« Noch hundert Jahre später hieß es in einer Baugeschichte Berlins über Langhans: »Ohne originell zu sein, verstand er in einer Zeit des gesunkenen Geschmackes, sich an edle Muster anzulehnen.«

Dies alles klingt recht mißgünstig, und es verkennt, daß Langhans bewußt der Begeisterung Johann Joachim Winckelmanns für das antike Griechenland folgte; dieser hatte die hellenistische Kunst als das eigentlich Schöpferische, als die wahre Klassik ausgerufen.

Ein Modell des Langhans-Tores wurde bei der öffentlichen Versammlung der Akademie der Künste zu Ehren der Schwester des Königs, Friederike Sophia Wilhelmine von Oranien-Nassau, am 16. August 1789 in Berlin gezeigt. Und vom 25. September desselben Jahres an konnten auch die Besucher einer öffentlichen Kunstausstellung der Akademie das Modell bewundern. Im Gegensatz zu mittelalterlichen Stadttoren, deren Aufgabe es war, Bollwerk gegen Feinde von außen zu sein, brachte die großzügige architektonische Gestalt des neuen Brandenburger Tores die Offenheit einer selbstbewußten Residenzstadt gegenüber der Außenwelt zum Ausdruck.

Der noch 1789 in Angriff genommene Bau (3) dürfte nach unterschiedlichen Schätzungen bis zu fünfhunderttausend Taler gekostet haben. Hunderttausende von Mauersteinen sowie riesige Mengen von Feld- und Kalksteinen wurden verbaut. Sächsischer Sandstein aus Cotta, Pirna und Postelwitz wurde auf dem Wasserwege herangeschafft. 1240 Quadratfuß Eisenblech wurden verarbeitet, 991 Fuhren Erde herbeigeschafft und 389 Fuhren Schutt abgefahren.

Im Auftrag des Hofes überwachte Minister v. Woellner den Bau, der auf wiederholten Befehl des Königs immer wieder beschleunigt werden mußte. Langhans selbst kümmerte sich trotz der Eile um jedes Detail. So schrieb er am 26. August 1789 an den Kaufmann Funicke: »Ich wäre nicht abgeneigt, zum Hauptgesims sogenannte Kettersteine zu nehmen, nur müssen selbige von der weißen Sorte seyn, die nicht verwittern.« Um die Steinmetzarbeiten zu schützen, waren aufwendige Kitt-, Öl- und Anstreicharbeiten vorgesehen. Da dem Minister v. Woellner jedoch die hierfür veranschlagte Summe von 1599 Talern und vier Groschen zu hoch erschien, bestimmte er, sämtliche Sandsteine mit einfachem Käsekitt zu verfugen und mit Lauge-Kalkfarbe abzufärben, was lediglich 1279 Taler und acht Groschen kosten würde.

Noch war das Tor gar nicht mit all seinem plastischen Schmuck versehen, als es nach zweijähriger Bauzeit ohne jede Feierlichkeit dem Verkehr übergeben wurde (4, 5). Das hierbei aufgenommene Protokoll besagt: »Actum, Berlin, den 6. August 1791. Nachdem auf Befehl Sr. Königl. Majestät die Passage in dem neu erbauten Brandenburger Thor heute eröffnet wurde, so bezog das daselbst wachthabende Militair die an diesem Thor neu erbaute Wache...« Weder wurde, wie später gemutmaßt, bei dieser Gelegenheit »Heil dir im Siegerkranz«, die nachmalige preußische Nationalhymne, gesungen, noch war der König anwesend – der paktierte zu diesem Zeitpunkt in Pillnitz mit Kaiser Leopold II.

Da steht es seitdem, das Brandenburger Tor. Mit einer Breite von 65,5 Metern, einer Tiefe von 11 Metern und einer Höhe, inklusive Quadriga, von ungefähr 26 Metern schließt es die Straße Unter den Linden und den Pariser Platz wuchtig und zugleich mit klarer Gliederung zum Tiergarten hin ab. Die monumentale, von zwei Flügelbauten eingefaßte Anlage besteht aus fünf Durchfahrten, die mittels massiver Querwände voneinander getrennt sind. Die Stirnseiten dieser Wände schmücken Sandsteinsäulen nach dorischem Vorbild – sechs auf jeder Torseite. Während die vier äußeren Durchfahrten eine Breite von jeweils 3,79 Metern haben, mißt die Mittelöffnung 5,50 Meter. Sie war ausschließlich den Mitgliedern des Hofes vorbehalten. Auf den Säulen ruhen ein dorisches Gebälk und eine Attika, auf der, durch einen Sockel nochmals hervorgehoben, später die Quadriga aufgestellt werden sollte.

Die bildhauerischen Arbeiten aus Sandstein, von Berliner und Potsdamer Künstlern ausgeführt, gehen zum großen Teil auf Entwürfe Johann Gottfried Schadows zurück, so die 32 kleinen Reliefs im Gebälk der beiden Längsseiten des Tores. Sie zeigen Kampfszenen zwischen Lapithen und Kentauren in Anlehnung an die Metopen des Parthenon in Athen. Das Flachrelief in der Attika-Mitte zur Stadtseite hin zeigt einen Zug der Friedensgöttin, nach einem von Schadow veränderten Entwurf Christian Bernhard Rodes (14). Dieses Relief beschrieb der Berliner Stadthistoriker Bogdan Krieger so: »Die Göttin des Friedens, mit einem Ölzweig und einem Lorbeerkranz in den Händen, sitzt auf einem von vier Putten gezogenen Triumphwagen. Vor dem Wagen gehen die Eintracht, die Freundschaft, die Staatsklugheit, die Siegesgöttin und die Tapferkeit, vor welcher die Zwietracht die Flucht nimmt. Dem Wagen folgen die Freude in tanzender Stellung mit einem Rosengürtel in den Händen, die Göttin des Überflusses... die Baukunst, die Malkunst, die Bildhauerkunst, die Göttin der höheren Wissenschaften nebst der Musik und Dichtung.«

An den Innenseiten der Durchfahrten sind zwanzig Reliefs mit Szenen aus der Herakles-Sage angebracht, von denen in diesem Buch einige Beispiele zu sehen sind (6–11). Das Flachrelief mit dem Zug der Friedensgöttin, die Metopenreliefs und der Herakleszyklus versinnbildlichen ebenso die Hoffnung auf eine die kriegerischen Zeiten ablösende Friedensperiode wie die Statuen des Mars, der sein Schwert in die Scheide steckt, und der Minerva (12, 13). Beide standen ursprünglich in stadtwärts gewandten Nischen zwischen Tor und Seitenflügeln. Beim Umbau des Brandenburger Tores 1868 wurden sie an ihren heutigen Standort, die seitlichen Außenwände des Torbaus, versetzt.

Dieser Schmuck wie auch die Quadriga fehlten noch, als am 22. Dezember 1792 die erste feierliche Prozession durch das neue Tor führte: Kronprinzessin Luise und ihre Schwester Friederike wurden als Bräute der beiden ältesten Söhne des Königs feierlich nach Berlin eingeholt. Zwei Jahre später schrieb Luise an ihren Bruder Georg: »Erinnerst Du Dich noch der Feier des heutigen Tages, wie bange mir wohl das Herz pochte, als ich den Toren Berlins näher kam und alle die Freuden- und Ehrenbezeigungen empfing... Ja, bester Freund, es war eine feierliche Stunde für mich, in der ich Berlins Einwohner ward.«

Die Quadriga

Zur Bekrönung des Torbaues entwarf Johann Gottfried Schadow 1789 die von Langhans als »Triumph des Friedens« vorgesehene Quadriga (15, 16). Schadow wurde am 20. Mai 1764 in Berlin geboren und starb am 27. Januar 1850 in seiner Vaterstadt. Hier erlernte er bis 1785 an der Königlichen Werkstatt bei Tassaert die Bildhauerei. Auch nutzte er die Ausbildungsmöglichkeiten der Kunstakademie. Nach einer Italienreise mit einem längeren Romaufenthalt kehrte er 1787 nach Berlin zurück und wurde, nachdem er zunächst Mitarbeiter der Königlichen Porzellanmanufaktur war, nach dem Tode Tassaerts 1788 Leiter der Hofbildhauerwerkstatt. Damit verbunden war das angesehene Amt eines »Direktors aller Skulpturen« beim von Langhans geleiteten Oberhofbauamt. 1815 wurde er Direktor der Berliner Akademie der Künste.

Schadow ist der bedeutendste deutsche Bildhauer um 1800. Unter seinen nahezu dreihundert Plastiken befinden sich so bekannte wie das Grabmal für den Grafen von der Mark, die Stettiner Marmorstatue Friedrichs II. sowie die berühmte Prinzessinnengruppe, das erste lebensgroße Doppelstandbild des Klassizismus, das die Schwestern Luise und Friederike von Mecklenburg-Strelitz darstellt.

Die handwerkliche Ausführung der Quadriga wurde dem Potsdamer Kupferschmied Emanuel Jury übertragen. Bereits am 13. März 1789 fand eine Konferenz mit Langhans, Schadow und Jury statt, bei der laut Protokoll unter anderem folgendes verhandelt wurde: »Nachdem sich der Kupferschmidt Jury weitläufig erkläret hatte, in welcher Art er mit seiner Arbeit zu werke gehen wolle und könne, wurde beschlossen, daß von Hr. Schadow ein Modell... zu fertigen sey, welches die Maaße einer Gruppe von 4 Pferde und einem Wagen nebst der Victoria deutlich ausdrückte, wornach sodenn das große Modell, dessen Pferde mit dem Kopf 10 Fuß hoch sein sollten, von Holz zum wahren Modell in der Größe gefertiget würden, wie die ganze Gruppe in natura sein sollte... Ohneerachtet Herr Jury in dieser ganzen Sache keine Schwierigkeiten findet, so träget er jedennoch dahin an, daß ihm entweder Englisches Kupfer, oder aber, wenn dieses nicht gegeben werden wolle, das beste hiesige Kupfer geliefert werde... Die Vergoldung anbelangend, so weiß er vor der Hand noch niemand hierzu vorzuschlagen...«

Mit der Fertigung der Holzmodelle wurden Vater und Sohn Wohler in Potsdam beauftragt. Die Vergoldung ist nicht zustande gekommen. Zwar wird im Verzeichnis der Kunstausstellung von 1793 im Zusammenhang mit dem Modell der Quadriga von einer Veredelung der Siegesgöttin »mit durchaus echtem Golde« gesprochen, doch erließ König Friedrich Wilhelm II. am 11. Juli 1793 aus dem Lager von Mainz an v. Woellner die folgende Kabinettsordre: »Ich... will daher, daß diese außerordentlich gutgerathende Quadriga nicht verguldet, sondern ihre natürliche Farbe behalte. Friedrich Wilhelm.«

Doch wir eilen der Zeit voraus. Zunächst legte Schadow sein besonderes Augenmerk auf den Entwurf der Pferde. Um die Bewegung der Tiere studieren zu können, wurde ein Stallmeister des Königlichen Marstalls angewiesen, dem Künstler Pferde vorzureiten, wonach dieser seine Zeichnungen machte. Offenbar ließ Schadow bei dem Entwurf der Siegesgöttin keine solche Sorgfalt walten, denn nach eigenen Aussagen fertigte er hierfür lediglich eine Skizze an (17, 18).

Die Ausführung der Quadriga dauerte länger als angenommen. Mehrfach mahnte Minister v. Woellner den Fortgang der Arbeiten an, ja, er ließ die Bildhauer Wohler und den Kupferschmied Jury sogar vernehmen. In einer schriftlichen Stellungnahme begründeten die Holzbildhauer den Verzug folgendermaßen: »Warum wir laut unsern Accort vom 6. 5. 1789 nicht gehörig betrieben hätten, in dem die Proportion der Pferde auf 10 Fuß ... festgesetzt wurde ... erhielten wir unter dem 19. Julius 89 den Befehl von dem Herrn Geheimdrath Langhans, daß sich ein Zweifel gefunden, und wir einhalten sollten, bis die Academie der Künste die Proportion zu der Grouppe bestimmt hätte. Unter dem 15. September 89 erhielten wir den Befehl, daß die Academie die Grouppe auf 12 Fuß höhe resolvirt hätte ... wir arbeiteten ohneracht, daß alles größer wurde, ein Pferd fertig.«

Die ganze Arbeit mußte also zwei Fuß größer, als ursprünglich geplant und bereits begonnen, ausgeführt werden. Auch Kupferschmied Emanuel Jury verwies bei seiner schriftlichen Rechtfertigung auf diese Änderung der Pläne und gab zu bedenken, daß »solche Colossus nur alle Jahrhunderte vorfallen und auch wegen der Größe nicht genau beurteilt und beaccordirt werden können«. Er bietet an, einen Teil der Arbeit in die Hände eines anderen Kupferschmieds legen zu lassen. Auf dieses Angebot gehen seine Auftraggeber ein, und sie übertragen die Anfertigung der Viktoria dem Klempnermeister Köhler aus Potsdam.

Im Frühsommer 1793 war es dann soweit. Am 15. Juni berichtet Jury, die Quadriga werde am folgenden Montag zu Wasser nach Berlin befördert und dort am Mittwochabend oder Donnerstag früh eintreffen. Kaum war das Kunstwerk in Berlin angekommen, als offizielle Stellen die Nacktheit der Viktoria monierten. So mußte ihr nachträglich ein Mantel geschmiedet werden, bei dessen Anbringung der Siegesgöttin die Beine abgesägt werden mußten.

In seinem Bericht vom 13. September 1793 an den Minister v. Woellner konnte Langhans vermelden, daß das Tor jetzt endgültig seiner Vollendung entgegengehe. Die Quadriga stünde an ihrem Platze, die Kupferschmiede seien nun mit der Wiederherstellung der Kupferbedachung beschäftigt. Die Fläche vor dem Tor sei planiert und würde mit Pflaster versehen. Auch machte Schadow Vorschläge für die Beleuchtung des Platzes. An den Rand des Berichts schrieb Minister v. Woellner: »Gottlob! daß wir endlich einmal so weit sind!«

Nun hatte man nur noch dafür Sorge zu tragen, daß das Tor geschlossen werden konnte. Für die mittlere Durchfahrt, die dem Hofe vorbehalten war, wurde ein hölzernes Tor angefertigt, daß des Nachts verriegelt wurde. Für die Seitendurchfahrten gab es Holztore für die Nacht und eiserne Torgitter, die in der Regel auch tagsüber geschlossen wurden, aber den Blick auf den Tiergarten nicht verdeckten. Sowohl die hölzernen als auch die eisernen Tore sollten sich in den folgenden Jahren als Anlaß ständigen Ärgernisses herausstellen. Bereits 1795 war die erste Reparatur fällig. In jenem Jahr kam es auch zu einem ersten Malheur, als ein Flügel des mittleren Tores vom Winde zugeworfen wurde, kaum daß der König es passiert hatte.

Doch es sollte noch schlimmer kommen. Am 4. November 1804 wird vom zuständigen Gouvernement der folgende Bericht erstellt: »Gestern Abend, als die Prinzessin Ferdinand von Preußen [gemeint ist die Gemahlin des Prinzen August Ferdinand] das Tor passierte, entriß der Sturm der einen Schildwache den Torflügel und schleuderte ihn gegen den Wagen, so daß der Wagen teils zerschmettert worden und noch größeres Unheil zu befürchten stand. Dieser Fall ist schon mehrere Male auch an anderen Toren bei starkem Winde gewesen und auch dem Prinzen August Ferdinand zweimal passiert, weil die Torflügel zu groß und schwer und die Schildwache, welche in einer Hand das Gewehr halten, nicht stark genug sind, dem Sturmwinde den erforderlichen Widerstand zu leisten. Das Bauamt wird ersucht irgendein Mittel ausfindig zu machen, um diesem Übel abzuhelfen, zumal es solcher schweren und hohen Tore nicht bedarf.« Doch es sollten noch Jahrzehnte vergehen, bis die Tore endgültig abgebaut wurden.

Die am Tor postierte Schildwache hatte wirklich keinen einfachen Dienst. Das bekam auch der Dichter und Naturforscher Adelbert v. Chamisso zu spüren, der hier seine Soldatenpflicht erfüllte. In einem Kommandanturbericht vom 8. Dezember 1804 heißt es: »Da die Wacht am Brandenburger Thor beim Einpassieren des Königs nicht in gehöriger Ordnung gewesen, und die Honneurs nicht gehörig gemacht wurden, so soll der Lieutenant von Chamisso, Regiments von Goetz, in Arrest und ans Regiment gemeldet werden ...« Und Jahre später schreibt die Tänzerin Lola Montez in ihren Memoiren: »Die Wache am Brandenburger Thore muß an einem Sonntage wahrlich ihre Noth haben. Es vergeht keine Minute, ohne daß sie entweder vor einer prinzlichen und fürstlichen Equipage oder vor einem Offizier die Honneurs machen müßte.«

1804 wurde die erste gründliche Ausbesserung des Brandenburger Tores nötig. Für eine Summe von 6500 Talern mußte das Bauwerk gereinigt, neu verkittet, geölt und angestrichen werden, wobei insbesondere die neue Farbe Kritik hervorrief. So schrieb der

Offizier und Schriftsteller Julius v. Voß im Jahre 1811 in seiner Schrift »Neu-Berlin oder vaterländische Ideen über Wiedergedeihen und Emporblühen dieser Hauptstadt«: »Das Brandenburger Thor können die Baumeister nicht auf sich beziehen, weil es eine Kopie ist, ihr Geist hat sich aber späterhin daran verkündet, wo sie, statt der weißen, den Marmor nachahmenden Farbe, die gegen das Baumgrün des Thiergartens so idealisch leuchtete, es mit einem ekelhaften Caffee au lait besudelten, das auch nicht einmal einer gemeinen Steingattung entspricht und dem Eingang in die schönste Straße von Europa alle Würde nahm.« Ein Mißstand, der in den nachfolgenden Jahren zum Glück beseitigt wurde.

Napoleon, der Pferdedieb

»Hier wollen wir stille stehen und das Brandenburger Tor und die darauf stehende Victoria betrachten. Die Göttin da oben wird ihnen aus der neuesten Geschichte genugsam bekannt sein. Die gute Frau hat auch ihre Schicksale gehabt. Man sieht's ihr nicht an, der mutigen Wagenlenkerin.« Im Jahre 1822, als Heinrich Heine dies schrieb, hatte die Viktoria in der Tat bereits einiges durchgemacht. Ihren ersten Schicksalsschlag hatte sie einem Kaiser zu verdanken: Napoleon. Ganz Europa hatte der Korse schon mit Krieg überzogen, als er in der Doppelschlacht bei Jena und Auerstedt am 14. Oktober 1806 dem Preußen Friedrich Wilhelm III. eine Niederlage bereitete, die für den jungen Staat und seine Armee das vorläufige Ende bedeutete. Der König flüchtete mit seiner Gemahlin Luise ins ferne Königsberg, die Garnison wurde aus der nicht mehr verteidigungsfähigen Hauptstadt abgezogen. Der Gouverneur, Graf Friedrich Wilhelm von der Schulenburg, ließ am 17. Oktober 1806 ein Plakat anschlagen, das die berühmt gewordenen Sätze enthielt: »Der König hat eine Bataille verlohren. Jetzt ist Ruhe die erste Bürgerpflicht.«

Wenige Tage darauf, am 27. Oktober, nachmittags um vier Uhr, durchritt Kaiser Napoleon das Brandenburger Tor (19). In der tags darauf erscheinenden »Vossischen Zeitung« las sich das Ereignis so: »Der Donner der Kanonen und das Geläute der Glocken verkündeten die Ankunft. Eine unermeßliche Menge Volks empfing Se. Kaiserl. Königl. Majestät mit den lebhaftesten Freudensbezeugungen. Se. Excellenz, der Herr General Hülin, Kommandant dieser Hauptstadt, stellten Sr. Majestät dem Kaiser die Mitglieder des Magistrats, den Adel u. die vornehmsten der Stadt vor, welche sich zu diesem Behuf nach dem Brandenburger Thor begeben hatten...« Bei diesem euphorischen Bericht muß allerdings berücksichtigt werden, daß die »Vossische Zeitung« unter französischer Kuratel stand. Nach anderen Überlieferungen nämlich war ein französischer Offizier zu den vor der Stadtseite des Tores aufgebauten Tribünen geritten und hatte den dort versammelten Honoratioren zugerufen, Seine Majestät habe angeordnet, daß die Herren bei seinem Vorbeiritt den Hut abzunehmen hätten, worauf ein Justizrat mit Namen Schmidt laut über den Platz rief: »Wir werden ihm etwas pfeifen!«

Die Berliner stöhnten unter der Last der nun folgenden Besetzung. Sie mußten den französischen Soldaten, Offizieren und Beamten Quartier gewähren. Am 1. November 1806 waren in Berliner Privathaushalten, öffentlichen Gebäuden und sonstigen zur Verfügung stehenden Räumen 60 000 Franzosen untergebracht, und das bei einer Bevölkerung von nur rund 170 000 Köpfen. Von Beginn des Jahres 1807 an mußten Bürger, die keine Unterkunft zur Verfügung stellten, Quartiergeld zahlen. Erst im Dezember 1808 zogen die Besatzer wieder ab.

Als besondere Demütigung für die Stadt befahl Napoleon, die Quadriga vom Brandenburger Tor herunterzunehmen und als Trophäe nach Paris zu bringen (20–22). Eine Abordnung mit Schadow an der Spitze versuchte, dies zu verhindern, und überreichte am 17. November 1806 eine Bittschrift an den Kaiser, doch ohne Erfolg. Noch am selben Tag notierte Schadow in einem Brief: »Mrs. Denon war vor einer Stunde bei mir, er zeigte mir an, der Kaiser habe befohlen, die Quadriga vom Brandenburgerthore abzunehmen und solche nach Frankreich zu schaffen, ich mußte ihm die Adresse von Jury geben, er geht morgen nach Potsdam und bringt diesen wahrscheinlich mit, um die Gruppe abzunehmen...«

Anfang Dezember 1806 verrichtete nun der Kupferschmied Emanuel Jury seine traurige Arbeit, nahm die Quadriga vom Tor und verpackte sie in zwölf Kisten, die am 21. Dezember zu Wasser über Hamburg nach Paris gebracht wurden. Mitte Mai 1807 traf das Beutegut zusammen mit anderen eroberten Kunstwerken in der Seinestadt ein. Im »Frankfurter Journal« vom 22. Mai 1807 ist zu lesen: »Man ist dabei, am St. Nicolashafen 80 oder 100 kolossale Kisten auszuschiffen, die Antiquitäten aus Berlin und Potsdam enthalten und die Quadriga, die man auf dem Brandenburger Tore in Berlin sah.«

Zunächst war es Napoleons Plan, die Quadriga auf einem noch zu erbauenden Triumphbogen aufstellen zu lassen, später bestimmte er, daß sie das Tor Saint Denis zu Paris schmücken sollte. Doch beide Pläne wurden nicht verwirklicht. Immerhin reparierte man die auf dem Transport erlittenen Beschädigungen.

In Berlin ragte derweil auf dem Brandenburger Tor die eiserne Stange in den Himmel, die der Viktoria zuvor als Stütze gedient hatte.

Einer wohl erfundenen Geschichte zufolge fragte der Lehrer und Turnvater Friedrich Ludwig Jahn damals einen seiner Schüler, was er beim Anblick des nackten Tores empfinde. Als dieser antwortete, er fühle nichts, soll Jahn ihn mit einer Ohrfeige und den Worten belehrt haben: »Du wirst in Zukunft daran denken, daß wir alles tun müssen, um die Quadriga zurückzuerhalten.«

Dies sollte noch einige Jahre dauern. Doch im Volk regte sich zunehmend Widerstand. In seinen berühmten »Reden an die deutsche Nation« forderte Johann Gottlieb Fichte die sittliche Erneuerung des Volkes, ein einiges, freies Vaterland sowie die Befreiung von der Fremdherrschaft. Das Brandenburger Tor und die entführte Quadriga wurden zum nationalen Symbol dieses Freiheitsstrebens. Aber erst die verheerende Niederlage von Napoleons Grande Armée in Rußland schuf die Voraussetzung für einen nationalen Befreiungskampf. 1813 schlossen sich Preußen, Rußland und Österreich zusammen. Die gemeinsam geführten Freiheitskriege gipfelten am 24. Oktober 1813 in der berühmten Völkerschlacht bei Leipzig, in der Napoleon vernichtend geschlagen wurde.

In Berlin druckte die Zeitschrift »Neue Fakkeln« Anfang 1814 folgendes Gedicht:

O! Friedrich Wilhelm, diesen Wagen
Laß ja dem Feinde nicht!
Wir bitten drum, und müßten wir selbst tragen
Sein centnerschwer Gewicht.
Und stehst du wieder auf dem Tor, du Wagen,
Dann schlagen dankend wir an unser Herz...

Diesem Wunsch kam der preußische General Blücher, den die Berliner »Marschall Vorwärts« nannten, nach. Er erwirkte die sofortige Rückgabe der Quadriga. Ihr Weg nach Hause wurde ein Triumphzug (23–26). Verpackt in fünfzehn Kisten, verladen auf sechs schwere Wagen, wurde sie von 52 Pferden über Brüssel und Aachen zunächst nach Düsseldorf gezogen, wo sie auf sechs Fähren über den Rhein gesetzt wurde. Von dort berichteten die »Berlinischen Nachrichten« am 19. Mai 1814: »Schon mehrere Stunden vorher war die ganze Gegend bei dem neuen Hafen mit Menschen bedeckt. Sobald man die Wagen, auf welchen jenes Kunstwerk transportirt wird, an dem jenseitigen Ufer des Rheins erblickte, wurden sie auf dem diesseitigen mit allgemeinem Jubelgeschrei bewillkommt und ... von den am Ufer stehenden versammelten Stadtbehörden unter Kanonendonner und unter dem Läuten aller Glocken empfangen ... Auf dem großen Platz in der Karlsstadt ward der Zug von der in Parade unter dem Gewehr stehenden Garnison mit militärischer Musik empfangen. Bei Endigung eines jeden Musikstückes ließ das Volk dem geliebten Könige Friedrich Wilhelm ein Vivat erschallen, dann, den verbündeten Monarchen – der gemeinschaftlichen Sache der Menschheit – und zuletzt allen, denen deutsches Blut in deutschen Adern rollt...«

Über und über bedeckt mit Kränzen, Girlanden, Gedichten und patriotischen Inschriften kam die Quadriga am 8. Juni in Zehlendorf an, wo sie im Hof des Jagdschlosses Grunewald ausgepackt und wieder zusammengesetzt wurde. Tausende begeisterte Menschen säumten den Weg, als das Viergespann anschließend nach Berlin gebracht wurde, um am 30. Juni an seinem angestammten Platz wieder aufgestellt zu werden. Zunächst jedoch verdeckte man die Gruppe mit einer zeltartigen Bedachung, da der König befohlen hatte, die Trophäe in der Hand der Siegesgöttin zu verändern. Nach einem Entwurf Karl Friedrich Schinkels wurde in der Werkstatt des Kupferschmieds Jury ein Eisernes Kreuz aus Kupferblech angefertigt, das am oberen Ende der Panierstange in einen Eichenkranz gesetzt wurde, über dem ein preußischer Adler seine Schwingen breitete (27). Nun war endgültig aus der Friedensgöttin Eirene die Siegesgöttin Viktoria geworden. Als König Friedrich Wilhelm III. an der Spitze seines siegreichen preußischen Heeres von Charlottenburg kommend am Brandenburger Tor angelangt war, wurde die zurückgekehrte Quadriga enthüllt (28). Man schrieb den 7. August 1814.

Berliner Biedermeier

Im Jahr 1815 wurde auf dem Wiener Kongreß die europäische Landkarte neu geordnet. Frieden kehrte ein, und nach den Jahren der Wirren und der Kriege hatte nun das Private, das scheinbar Unpolitische den Vorrang. Es war die Zeit des Biedermeier, Jahre zwischen Romantik und Realismus, zwischen religiösem Schwärmertum und nationaler Ernüchterung.

Zum geselligen Leben jener Jahre gehörte, was die Berliner betraf, der Ausflug in den Tiergarten (29–35). Das bunte Treiben dort beschreibt E.T.A. Hoffmann zu Beginn seines »Ritter Gluck«: »Der Spätherbst in Berlin hat gewöhnlich noch einige schöne Tage. Die Sonne tritt freundlich aus dem Gewölk hervor, und schnell verdampft die Nässe in der lauen Luft, welche durch die Straßen weht. Dann sieht man eine lange Reihe, buntgemischt – Elegants, Bürger mit der Hausfrau und den lieben Kleinen in Sonntagskleidern, Geistliche, Jüdinnen, Referendare, Freudenmädchen, Professoren, Putzmacherinnen, Tänzer, Offiziere usw. durch die Linden nach dem Tiergarten ziehen.« Und der Dichter Moritz Saphir schrieb in seiner »Fahrt nach Charlottenburg«: ». . . und so fuhr ich denn . . . gerade zum Tore hinaus, auf welchem die Viktoria, schön wie der Sieg und glänzend wie die Erinnerung an alle Siege, in denen der Preuß' den Preis davon trug, im herrlichen Schimmer dastand. Es kann keinen imposanteren Anblick geben, als wenn die sinkende Sonne das Haupt dieser Göttin vergoldet und sie in einer Strahlenkrone verklärt dasteht und durch die majestätischen Säulen des hohen Tores die rosichte Abendflut hereinleuchtet. . .«

In dieser Zeit bekam das Geviert zwischen dem Brandenburger Tor und der Straße Unter den Linden, das bisher wegen seiner Form »Quarré« genannt worden war, in Erinnerung an den Sieg über Napoleon seinen heutigen Namen: Pariser Platz.

Im Jahre 1816 mußte das Brandenburger Tor wieder einmal renoviert werden. Für 1318 Taler, zwei Silbergroschen und zehn Pfennige wurden Reparaturen durchgeführt. Eines besonderen Problems nahm sich die Ministerialbaukommission mit Schreiben vom 14. März 1824 an das Polizeipräsidium an. Dieses wurde ersucht, »gegen die Verunreinigung dieses so schönen Bauwerks zweckdienliche Maßregeln zu treffen«. Hintergrund des Briefes war das zunehmende Anheften von Plakaten an die Säulen des Tores. Das machte sich nicht gut, zumal bei Anlässen wie dem am 28. November 1823, als der spätere König Friedrich Wilhelm IV. seine Braut, Prinzessin Elisabeth von Bayern, eben dort am Brandenburger Tor empfangen hatte. Und so kam am 1. April 1824 vom Polizeipräsidium die Weisung, daß der Kommandant die Wachen anzuhalten habe, jedes Ankleben von Plakaten an die Säulen zu verhindern. Zudem wurde in den Zeitungen der Stadt ein Hinweis veröffentlicht, daß Zuwiderhandlungen mit einem Taler Bußgeld oder »verhältnismäßiger Leibesstrafe« geahndet werden würden.

Am 11. Juni 1840 fand im Berliner Dom der Trauergottesdienst für den am 7. Juni verstorbenen König Friedrich Wilhelm III. statt. Die anschließende nächtliche Überführung des Sarges zum Mausoleum im Charlottenburger Schloßpark schilderte ein Zeitgenosse wie folgt: »Um 11 Uhr setzte sich der Zug in Bewegung . . . Die Luft war völlig windstill; kein Gas erleuchtete die Straßen; ein leicht bewölkter Mond verbreitete ein elegisches Dämmerlicht; die zahllosen Volksmassen beobachteten eine rührende Stille. Ein bewegliches Spalier von Garde du Corps und Ulanen hielt einen breiten Weg frei. Der Zug ging durch die mittlere Promenade der Linden, die sonst jedem Wagen verschlossen ist; Pferde und Wagen bewegten sich auf dieser ungepflasterten Straße völlig lautlos, und die wenigen Fackeln erhellten um so magischer die eng zusammengeneigten Wipfel der Bäume. So durchschritt der Trauerzug die Mitte des Brandenburger Thores, um langsam und gemessen den dunkel beschatteten, in seiner ganzen Ausdehnung von ruhigen Volksmassen erfüllten Weg zurückzulegen.«

Eine Epoche war zu Ende gegangen, doch der Regierungsantritt Friedrich Wilhelms IV. war mit um so größeren politischen Erwartungen verknüpft. Der junge König schien diese zunächst auch zu rechtfertigen: Er amnestierte politisch Verfolgte, milderte die Zensur und gewährte den aus Göttingen verjagten Brüdern Jacob und Wilhelm Grimm in Berlin Asyl und eine neue Wirkungsstätte an der Akademie der Wissenschaften. Doch ein bereits 1815 gegebenes Verfassungsversprechen einzulösen, zeigte er sich nicht gewillt. Und so dauerte es nicht lange, bis es im März 1848 zur Eskalation kam, zur Revolution. Ausgelöst durch die Februarrevolution in Frankreich, die dort zur Ausrufung der Republik geführt hatte, kam es in den deutschen Staaten zu Unruhen. Viele Berliner versammelten sich zu politischen Kundgebungen vor den Toren der Stadt, vor allem in den »Zelten« im Tiergarten. Etwa zehntausend Demonstranten zogen am 14. März 1848 von dort durch das Brandenburger Tor in Richtung Schloß, um in einer »Adresse an den König« ihre Forderungen nach politischen Reformen zu überreichen.

Doch dazu kam es nicht. Kavallerie trieb die Demonstranten mit dem flachen Säbel auseinander. Die Lage verschärfte sich, überall in der Stadt wurden Barrikaden gebaut. Dann, am 18. März, fielen Schüsse. Bilanz: 19 gefallene Soldaten und 183 Tote auf seiten der aufständischen Bürger. Nun erst lenkte der König ein. Am 21. März ritt er mit einer schwarz-rot-goldenen Armbinde durch die Stadt. Er bewilligte eine verfassunggebende Versammlung in Preußen und versprach, sich die Ziele der deutschen Bewegung, Freiheit und Einheit, zu eigen zu machen.

Die scheinbare Idylle des Biedermeiers war abrupt zu Ende gegangen.

Drei Kriege

1861 war Wilhelm I. seinem verstorbenen Bruder auf dem preußischen Königsthron gefolgt. Hatte zunächst vor allem das liberale Berlin große politische Hoffnungen auf ihn gesetzt, so kam es bald zu tiefgreifenden Verstimmungen, etwa in der Frage der Berufung des einstigen Revolutionsgegners Otto v. Bismarck zum Ministerpräsidenten. Doch ein außenpolitischer Konflikt band die widerstrebenden politischen Kräfte und überbrückte die inneren Probleme. Um die Zukunft Schleswig-Holsteins kam es 1864 zum Krieg gegen Dänemark, den die Deutschen bei den Düppeler Schanzen für sich entschieden.

Theodor Fontane war Augenzeuge des Triumphzugs der Sieger am 7. Dezember 1864 am Pariser Platz (36):

»Wer kommt? wer? —
Fünf Regimenter von Düppel her.
Fünf Regimenter vom dritten Korps
Rücken durchs Brandenburger Tor;
Prinz Friedrich Karl, Wrangel, Manstein,
General Roeder, General Canstein,
Fünf Regimenter, vom Sundewitt
Rücken sie an in Schritt und Tritt.«

Das Gedicht »Einzug« endet, als die Parade das Friedrich-Denkmal Unter den Linden erreicht:

»Alles still, kein Pferdegeschnauf,
Zehntausend blicken zu ihm auf;
Der neigt sich leise und lüpft den Hut:
›Konzediere, es war gut!‹«

Der siegreich bestandene deutsch-dänische Krieg stärkte die auf die deutsche Einigung unter preußischer Führung gerichteten Kräfte. Preußens Gewicht nahm ständig zu. Zugleich begann seit der Mitte des 19. Jahrhunderts die preußische Hauptstadt im Zuge der fortschreitenden Industrialisierung und einer raschen Bevölkerungszunahme rapide zu wachsen und ihre alten Grenzen zu sprengen.

Zum 1. Januar 1861 wurden zahlreiche Eingemeindungen im Süden, Westen und Nordwesten Berlins vorgenommen. Das Stadtgebiet vergrößerte sich, die Stadtmauer und ihre alten Tore wurden überflüssig. Zudem behinderten sie den zunehmenden Verkehr und die Bautätigkeit in der prosperierenden Stadt. Durch den deutsch-dänischen Krieg verzögerten sich die geplanten Abrißmaßnahmen bis in das Jahr 1865. Dann jedoch war es soweit: Mauer und Stadttore fielen der Spitzhacke zum Opfer. Einzig das Brandenburger Tor blieb erhalten, jedoch sollte es bauliche Veränderungen erfahren.

Am 9. November 1865 erließ der Minister für Handel, Gewerbe und öffentliche Arbeiten, Graf Heinrich August Friedrich von Itzenplitz, folgende Verfügung: »Die Königl. Ministerial-Bau-Kommission wird veranlaßt, ein durch Zeichnungen veranschaulichtes Projekt darüber aufzustellen, wie das Torgebäude des Brandenburger Tores nach dem Abbruch der Stadtmauer zum Abschluß zu bringen ist, damit es auch vom Tiergarten aus einen angemessenen und würdigen Anblick gewähre. Es ist dabei festzuhalten, daß die monumentalen Flügelgebäude, welche einen integrierenden Teil des Vorgebäudes bilden, beizubehalten, dagegen die mittleren Anbauten, in welchen Ställe angebracht sind, vielleicht abzubrechen sind...«

Schon am 26. Dezember desselben Jahres legte Bauinspektor Hermann Blankenstein der Ministerialbaukommission sechs Entwürfe und einen Bericht vor, der Vorschläge für eine Umgestaltung der seitlichen

Anbauten des Tores unterbreitete. Einleitend heißt es dort über das Bauwerk: »Da es auch seiner Architektur nach das bedeutendste ist und gleichzeitig den Zugang zu der prächtigsten Straße Berlins bildet, so erscheint es billig, es so umzubauen und zu schmücken, wie es sich für ein Haupt- und Prachttor der Residenz geziemt...« Blankenstein plädierte dafür, beiderseits des Tores zwischen diesem und den angrenzenden Flügelbauten Durchbrüche herzustellen, und fuhr dann fort: »Der Unterzeichnete ist dabei von der Ansicht geleitet worden, nicht nur den Bedürfnissen des Verkehrs Rechnung zu tragen und der ganzen Bauanlage eine einheitliche Gestalt zu geben, sondern auch ihr einen gemeinsamen monumentalen Gedanken unterzulegen, damit das Tor nicht als ein müßiger Schmuck, sondern als ein Denkmal vaterländischer Geschichte erscheine. Im Volksbewußtsein gilt das Brandenburger Tor wegen der an der Wiedereroberung der Victoria sich knüpfenden Erinnerungen ungeachtet seiner früheren Entstehung längst als Denkmal des Befreiungskrieges...«

Es soll hier darauf verzichtet werden, die Blankensteinschen Entwürfe im einzelnen vorzustellen, denn das Ministerium lehnte sie alle ab und beauftragte die Ministerialbaukommission, ein neues Projekt auszuarbeiten. Ausdrückliche Vorgabe war dabei, »die beiden symbolischen Figuren« — gemeint sind die Standbilder der Minerva und des Mars —, »welche auf der Stelle der durchzubrechenden Öffnungen stehen, anderweitig schicklich anzubringen«. Ein hierauf vorgelegter Plan des Geheimen Oberhofbaurats Johann Heinrich Strack fand schließlich die Zustimmung sowohl des Ministers Graf Itzenplitz als auch des Königs. Die benötigten 5900 Taler für die Arbeiten waren bereits bewilligt, als man den Umbau erneut aufschieben mußte.

Inzwischen war es über die Frage der Vorherrschaft im Deutschen Bund, der 1815 an die Stelle des von Napoleon zerstörten alten Reiches getreten war, zum Krieg zwischen Preußen und Österreich gekommen, den das Habsburger Reich verlor. Mittlerweile schon der Tradition entsprechend, sollte das siegreiche preußische Heer durch das Brandenburger Tor in der Hauptstadt Einzug halten. Doch es gab ein Problem: Die eisernen Torflügel waren bereits 1840 abgebaut worden, das Tor war seitdem nicht mehr verschließbar. Und so wurde auf dem Polizeipräsidium mit Datum vom 14. September 1866 das folgende Schreiben an die Ministerialbaukommission verfaßt: »Zur Sicherung des Einzuges der Truppen am 20. und 21. September, insbesondere auch um Störungen des Vorbeimarsches derselben vor Sr. Majestät dem Könige zu vermeiden, ist es erforderlich, das Brandenburger Tor sofort nach dem Durchzug der Truppen zu schließen, den Straßendurchlaß zwischen dem Tor und dem Steuergebäude durch einen starken Zaun aber ganz zu sperren. Da dem Vernehmen nach die beiden Torflügel nicht mehr vorhanden sind, wird die Ministerial-Bau-Kommission ersucht, für die fünf Öffnungen des Tores interimistische, genügend starke und mindestens 8 Fuß hohe verschließbare Flügeltore des Schleunigsten anbringen zu lassen...«

Fieberhaft wurden Tor und Stadt geschmückt. Theodor Fontane schilderte die festliche Stimmung dieser großen Tage in seinem Buch »Der deutsche Krieg von 1866«: »Am 20. früh... stand die Stadt in festlichem Empfangsschmucke da. Das Terrain, auf dem der Einzug stattfinden sollte, war selbstverständlich die breite, plätzereiche Avenue zwischen dem Brandenburger Thor und dem Schloß... Bereits um 9 Uhr Vormittags war die Festesstraße von hin und her wogenden, festlich gekleideten Menschenmassen gefüllt. Namentlich bot der Pariser Platz mit den ringsum emporsteigenden, Kopf an Kopf besetzten Tribünen ein überaus prächtiges und belebtes Bild. Die Fenster an den öffentlichen und Privatgebäuden waren von Schaulustigen dicht besetzt, ja selbst die Dächer bis an den First waren Kopf an Kopf bedeckt; ebenso waren die Bäume Unter den Linden von Neugierigen occupirt. Um 11 Uhr erschien der König... vor seinem Palais. Von den Prinzen und der Suite begleitet, ritt er auf der ›Sadowa‹ die Linden entlang, nach allen Seiten hin huldreich dem enthusiastischen Jubel dankend. Dieser schwoll zu einem Sturm der Begeisterung... sobald er den Pariser Platz erreicht hatte... Von diesem Jubel begleitet, passirte der König das Brandenburger Thor nach außen zu und sprengte vor die Front seiner Truppen... Gleich darauf eröffnete Feldmarschall Graf Wrangel, an der Spitze der Generalität, den Einzug.« (37).

Als die Festtage beendet waren und sich die Menschen verlaufen hatten, konnte mit dem Umbau des Tores begonnen werden. Für wie bedeutend diese Maßnahme angesehen wurde, wird dadurch deutlich, daß der König selbst sich um Detailfragen kümmerte. So erließ er am 28. Januar 1867 die folgende Kabinettsordre: »Auf Ihren Bericht vom 4. Dezember v. J. [vorigen Jahres]... genehmige Ich, daß die an das Brandenburger Tor zu Berlin angebauten niedrigen Ställe und Remisengebäude abgebrochen und die Flügelgebäude dieses Tores nach Maßgabe der beifolgenden Zeichnung C verlängert, auf den Rückseiten mit einer Säulenreihe versehen und mit den dahinterstehenden Steuer- und Wachtgebäuden durch Architrave und eine Glasbedachung in Verbindung gebracht werden. Wilhelm.«

Und so wurden die Gebäudeteile, die das Brandenburger Tor mit seinen beiden Flügelbauten verbunden hatten, beseitigt und durch Säulenhallen ersetzt, die beiderseits des Tores den Durchblick auf den Tiergarten gestatteten. Die der Stadt zugewandten Nischen, in denen bislang die Statuen von Mars und Minerva gestanden hatten, verschwanden; die beiden Plastiken erhielten neue Standorte im Innern der Säulenhallen, an den Schmalseiten des Tores.

1868 waren die Arbeiten beendet, das Tor war für die nächste Parade gerüstet. Und die sollte nicht lange auf sich warten lassen. Die Gründung des Norddeutschen Bundes unter Preußens Vorherrschaft hatte Deutschlands Einigung einen großen Schritt näherrücken lassen. Frankreich sah diese Entwicklung bei seinem östlichen Nachbarn mit großem Unbehagen. Französisch-preußische Spannungen wegen der Haltung Preußens in der Frage der spanischen Thronfolge führten schließlich am 9. Juli 1870 zur Kriegserklärung Frankreichs.

Nur anderthalb Monate später, am 2. September 1870, wurden die Franzosen in der Schlacht von Sedan vernichtend geschlagen. »Welch eine Wendung durch Gottes Führung« telegrafierte Wilhelm I. seiner Frau. Dieser Satz sollte ein Vierteljahrhundert später, zur 25-Jahrfeier der Schlacht von Sedan, das Brandenburger Tor schmücken (44). Am 18. Januar 1871 fand im Spiegelsaal des Schlosses von Versailles die Kaiserproklamation statt. Bismarck hatte sein Ziel erreicht, Deutschland war geeint. Am 16. Juni 1871 hielten zum dritten Mal innerhalb von sieben Jahren siegreiche preußische Truppen ihren Einzug in Berlin (38, 39).

»Wer diese feierlichen, großen und erhabenen Stunden nicht miterlebt hat«, berichtete ein Augenzeuge, »kann die stolze Seligkeit, das überschäumende Glücksgefühl, das die Stadt ergriffen hatte, nicht verstehen. Vom Dache eines Hauses am Pariser Platz... habe ich's mitangesehen, dieses Schauspiel ohnegleichen. Sehe noch von eitel Sonne übergossen die ungeheuren, unabsehbaren Menschenknäuel, die Tribünen, die Masten, den Fahnenwald, die Girlanden, die Ehrenpforten... [und die] Menschen, strahlende, selige, jauchzende Menschen... Bismarck, lorbeerbekränzt, reitet zwischen Moltke und Roon durch das Brandenburger Tor. Und hinter den drei weltgeschichtlichen Gestalten, die das Deutsche Reich geschmiedet haben, wird der Kaiser sichtbar, der Kronprinz, dessen ältester Sohn, der zwölfjährige Prinz Wilhelm... [und] ein Meer von Kornblumen und Maiglocken und Rosen ergießt sich über sie. Die Salven vom Lustgarten donnern herüber, von allen Kirchtürmen tönen die Glocken, die Musikkorps intonieren ›Nun danket alle Gott‹...«

Der deutsche Patriotismus hatte seinen absoluten Höhepunkt erreicht, man bejubelte Deutschlands gewonnenen Krieg. Geradezu prophetisch mutet es an, wenn Theodor Fontane, der auch diesen Einzug der siegreichen Truppen mit einem Gedicht würdigte, mit folgenden Zeilen schließt:

»Bei dem Fritzen-Denkmal stehen sie wieder,
Sie blicken hinauf, der Alte blickt nieder:
Er neigt sich leise über den Bug:
›Bon soir, Messieurs, nun ist es genug.‹«

Vierzig Jahre Frieden

Der Reichsgründung folgte eine Epoche des wirtschaftlichen Aufstiegs, die »Gründerzeit«. Wilhelm I., der nur zögernd die kaiserliche Würde angenommen hatte, wurde mit jedem Tag mehr zu einer Legende seiner selbst. Das Volk verehrte ihn, nannte ihn Wilhelm »den Großen«. Wenn er seine Ausfahrten in den Tiergarten unternahm, liefen die Menschen zusammen und ließen ihn hochleben (40).

Am 9. März 1888 starb der alte Kaiser, nur wenige Tage vor seinem 91. Geburtstag. Am 16. März fand die Trauerfeier im Berliner Dom statt. »Vale senex imperator« — Lebe wohl, alter Kaiser — stand in großen Buchstaben am schwarzverhangenen Brandenburger Tor unterhalb der Quadriga (41, 42). Als der Leichenzug das Tor durchquerte, konnte niemand in der vieltausendköpfigen Menge ahnen, daß er sich schon bald zu einer weiteren Trauerfeier würde einfinden müssen: Wilhelms Nachfolger, Friedrich III., starb, nach nur 99tägiger Regentschaft, am 15. Juni 1888. Noch am selben Tage trat sein Sohn als Kaiser Wilhelm II. im Alter von nur 29 Jahren die Nachfolge an. Das wilhelminische Zeitalter hatte begonnen.

Berlin wuchs und wuchs. Hatte die Stadt 1878 gerade die Millionengrenze überschritten, so zählte sie knapp dreißig Jahre später, 1905, bereits über zwei Millionen Einwohner. Dieses explosive Bevölkerungswachstum führte zur raschen Ausdehnung der Stadt; insbesondere im Westen entstanden vornehme großbürgerliche Wohngegenden und Boulevards wie etwa der Kurfürstendamm, der den »Linden« ein wenig von ihrem alten Glanz nahm. »Man« wohnte in Berlin W (wie West). Doch die Staatsbesuche wurden weiterhin in Berlin C (wie Centrum) empfangen, und zwar am Brandenburger Tor. 1889 und 1892 war es König Humbert von Italien, 1900 der alte Kaiser Franz Joseph von Österreich, 1902 wiederum ein italienischer König, diesmal Viktor Emanuel. Es folgten das schwedische, das englische und das dänische Königspaar.

Auch die alte Sitte der Einholung fürstlicher Bräute war nicht in Vergessenheit geraten. Am 3. Juni 1905 wurde Kronprinzessin Cäcilie am Tor empfangen, und am 26. Februar 1906 holte Prinz Eitel Friedrich seine Braut, die Herzogin Charlotte, hier nach Berlin. Vielleicht war es eine Art Gegenreaktion auf diesen Reigen feierlicher Haupt- und Staatsaktionen, daß der Berliner Volksmund damals von der Quadriga als der »vierspännigen Normaldroschke« sprach (47).

Der Pariser Platz, war von Beginn an das, was man eine feine Adresse nennt (46). Hier lebten im Lauf der Zeit der französische Gesandte in Berlin, die Familie des Musikers und Komponisten Giacomo Meyerbeer, Fürst Blücher, der Maler Edward Francis Cunningham, der Hofzimmermeister und Stadtrat Sommer sowie die Familie des Kaufmanns Louis Liebermann, dessen Sohn, der Maler Max Liebermann, das Haus am Pariser Platz Nr. 7, von den Linden aus gesehen rechts vom Tor, bis zu seinem Tode 1935 bewohnt hat.

Max Liebermann kehrte nach dem Tode seines Vaters im Jahre 1894 von längeren Auslandsaufenthalten nach Berlin zurück, um das elterliche Haus in Besitz zu nehmen. Sogleich beauftragte er den Architekten Hans Grisebach mit Planungen für ein Atelier auf dem Dach des Hauses. Am 29. Mai 1894 wurde unter Vorlage der Pläne ein entsprechender Antrag bei der Baupolizei eingereicht. Doch drei Wochen später schickte die zuständige Baukommission ein Schreiben an den Polizeipräsidenten, in dem es hieß: »Daß das projektierte Atelier eine entscheidende Verunschönerung des Brandenburger Tores bilden wird, indem die Monumentalität des Gesamtbildes schwer darunter leiden wird, dürfte wohl anzunehmen sein.« Die Erlaubnis zum Ausbau des Daches wurde versagt.

Am 7. März 1896 reichte Grisebach ein neues Baugesuch ein, da Liebermann »zur Ausübung seines Berufes jetzt ein Mietsatelier benutzen« müsse. Eine abermalige Ablehnung wurde wenige Wochen später zurückgezogen, da man fürchtete, das Bauverbot bei einem eventuellen Prozeß nicht durchsetzen zu können. Doch die Streitsache fand damit kein Ende, man konnte sich nicht auf eine Höhe für das Atelier einigen, und so wurde der Fall schließlich durch den Minister für Öffentliche Arbeiten, Karl. v. Thielen, an den Hof weitergereicht. Von dort erhielt er mit Datum vom 11. Februar 1897 folgende Anwort des Chefs des Zivilkabinetts: »Seine Majestät der Kaiser und König vermögen sich mit den Ausführungen des Berichtes Eurer Exzellenz vom 25. v. Mts. [vorigen Monats] betreffend die baupolizeiliche Erlaubnis zur Herstellung eines Malerateliers im 3. Stockwerk des Hauses Pariser Platz No. 7 nicht einverstanden zu erklären...« Dem Schreiben beigefügt war eine Bauskizze, auf der der Kaiser persönlich den eingezeichneten Atelierbau durchgestrichen und mit der Bemerkung »Scheußlich« versehen hatte. In Unkenntnis dieser Allerhöchsten Willensäußerung prozessierte Liebermann gegen das Bauverbot und erhielt in der zweiten Instanz recht. Am 22. April 1898 wurde ein neues Baugesuch genehmigt, Liebermann konnte sein Atelier bauen.

Beinahe wäre die Einrichtung des Ateliers auf dem Liebermannschen Haus nicht die einzige Baumaßnahme am Pariser Platz geblieben, denn mit Beginn des neuen Jahrhunderts meinte man, dem pulsierenden Großstadtverkehr neue Wege bahnen zu müssen. Es entstanden Pläne, die Gebäude links und rechts vom Brandenburger Tor umzubauen, mit Durchfahrten zu versehen oder gar ganz zu beseitigen. In einer Ausgabe der »Berliner Illustrirten Zeitung« aus dem Jahre 1908 heißt es: »Der Pariser Platz mit dem Brandenburger Tor in Berlin soll umgestaltet werden. Der Gedanke ist plötzlich aufgetaucht, und nun spricht man schon davon, als ob die Umgestaltung schon eine dringende Notwendigkeit wäre, obzwar auf dem Pariser Platz von einer Verkehrsüberlastung nichts zu spüren ist. Wenn nun durchaus umgestaltet werden muß, so wäre jedenfalls ein Projekt vorzuziehen, das so wenig als möglich das Brandenburger Tor in seiner heutigen Gestalt verändert...« Die Akademie des Bauwesens lud zu einem Ideenwettbewerb ein, und angesichts der eingereichten Vorschläge kann man von Glück sagen, daß die Pläne nie verwirklicht worden sind (49–53). Das Brandenburger Tor und der Pariser Platz blieben auch ohne Umbau dem Verkehr gewachsen.

Noch zweimal diente der Langhans-Bau als grandiose Kulisse für Inszenierungen imperialen Glanzes: Im Mai 1913 bei der Hochzeit der Kaisertochter Viktoria Luise mit dem Welfenprinzen Ernst August, Herzog zu Braunschweig und Lüneburg, und im Juni desselben Jahres aus Anlaß der Feierlichkeiten zum 25jährigen Regierungsjubiläum Kaiser Wilhelms II. (58, 59). Der gesamte europäische Hochadel besuchte aus diesen beiden Anlässen die Stadt. Unter den Gästen waren auch Zar Nikolaus II. von Rußland und George V., König von England. Noch war Frieden. Doch nur ein Jahr später fielen in Sarajevo die Schüsse, die einen Weltbrand auslösen sollten.

Fehlstart einer Republik

Am 1. August 1914 begann mit der deutschen Kriegserklärung an Rußland der Erste Weltkrieg (60). Was ein kurzer, siegreicher Feldzug werden sollte, wurde ein vierjähriges Völkerringen, das Millionen von Menschen das Leben kostete und in Deutschland das Zeitalter der Monarchie beendete. Als der Krieg ausbrach, waren Begeisterung und Opferbereitschaft des Volkes groß. Doch die militärischen Erfolge wurden immer seltener, die Versorgungslage im Reich verschlechterte sich zunehmend, und der Widerstand der Bevölkerung gegen eine Fortsetzung des Krieges wuchs. Sozialisten und Kommunisten, die die rasche Beendigung der Kampfhandlungen forderten, stießen auf wachsende Sympathien. Es kam zu Meutereien und schließlich zur Revolution. Am 9. November 1918 verkündete Reichskanzler Prinz Max v. Baden: »Der Kaiser und König hat sich entschlossen, dem Throne zu entsagen.« Der Krieg war verloren. Wilhelm II. floh nach Holland. Dem Sozialdemokraten Friedrich Ebert wurde das Reichskanzleramt übertragen.

In Berlin brodelte es. Aufständische zogen mit roten Fahnen durch die Stadt. Gleich zweimal wurde an jenem 9. November ein neuer Staat ausgerufen: Während der Sozialdemokrat Philipp Scheidemann vom Balkon des Reichstagsgebäudes die Deutsche Republik proklamierte, ließ der Kommunist Karl Liebknecht vom Balkon des Schlosses aus eine Freie Sozialistische Republik Deutschland hochleben. In den kommenden Wochen und Monaten zogen im fast täglichen Wechsel Formationen radikalisierter Kräfte von links und rechts durch das Brandenburger Tor: heimkehrende Soldaten und Spartakisten, Demonstranten jedweder Couleur und monarchistisch gesonnene Freikorps (63–66). Immer wieder kam es zu bürgerkriegsähnlichen Ausschreitungen und blutigen Schießereien, bei denen mitunter auch der mächtige Torbau als Gefechtsstand diente (67, 68). Dann wieder, am 3. März 1919, meldete sich unter dem Jubel der Berliner Bevölkerung auf dem eben noch umkämpften Pariser Platz die Schutztruppe aus Deutsch-Ostafrika zurück, angeführt von General Paul v. Lettow-Vorbeck und Gouverneur Heinrich Schnee (69).

Einen letzten Höhepunkt erreichten die Wirrnisse jener Tage im März 1920, als die Spartakisten ein weiteres Mal versuchten, den Staat in ihre Gewalt zu bekommen. Am 13. März zog als Gegenwehr die Marinebrigade Ehrhardt, Musikkorps und Reichskriegsflagge vorneweg, durch das Brandenburger Tor (73) und löste den Putschversuch des ostpreußischen Generallandschaftsdirektors Wolfgang Kapp aus, der jedoch bereits nach wenigen Tagen scheiterte. Beim Auszug der Putschtruppen am 18. März kam es, wiederum am Brandenburger Tor, zu einem blutigen Zwischenfall, als die nervös gewordenen Soldaten in die Menge der Schaulustigen schossen. Zwölf Tote und dreißig Verletzte waren zu beklagen (74).

Nachdem dann auch der Spartakisten-Aufstand niedergeschlagen worden war, konnte Berlin allmählich wieder zur Tagesordnung übergehen, allerdings zu der hektischen, oft chaotischen Tagesordnung der zwanziger Jahre: wirtschaftliche Prosperität und ein bedeutender Aufschwung des kulturellen Lebens auf der einen Seite, Inflation, Massenarbeitslosigkeit, Skandale, Attentate und maßlose Radikalisierung und Polarisierung auf der anderen.

Die Anlässe, zu denen das Brandenburger Tor die festliche Kulisse bildete, wurden in den Jahren der Weimarer Republik seltener. Kein Kaiser mehr, der durch die Mitteldurchfahrt des Portals ritt, keine Einholung von Prinzessinnen, kaum mehr große Militärparaden. Doch immerhin: Am 11. Mai 1925 hielt der neue Reichspräsident Paul v. Hindenburg durch das

Tor Einzug in die Stadt, und auch die Staatsbesuche jener Jahre — so 1928 der Schah von Afghanistan und 1929 der ägyptische König Fuad — betraten die Reichshauptstadt durch das Brandenburger Tor (78).

Zuvor schon, im Sommer 1926, mußte der Torbau einer Generalrenovierung unterzogen werden. Dazu hatte man ihn mit einem kompakten Holzgerüst versehen, das auch die Quadriga umgab (75). Der Volksmund sprach von »Berlins höchstem Pferdestall«. Doch Pferde waren selten geworden. Automobile hatten sie verdrängt, Taxis die Droschken abgelöst. Dieser Umbruch seines Gewerbes veranlaßte den Lohnkutscher Gustav Hartmann 1928 zu einer sensationellen Droschkenfahrt von Berlin nach Paris und zurück. Die Presse der Stadt stellte das Völkerverbindende dieser Reise groß heraus. Schließlich waren die Wunden des Ersten Weltkrieges noch nicht verheilt, und nur mühsam gelang es den Außenministern der vormaligen Erzfeinde Frankreich und Deutschland, Aristide Briand und Gustav Stresemann, ein erträgliches Nebeneinander ihrer beiden Völker herbeizuführen. Als Kutscher Hartmann, der »Eiserne Gustav«, durch das Brandenburger Tor nach Berlin zurückkehrte, erlebte der Pariser Platz einen Massenauflauf von Schaulustigen wie schon lange nicht mehr (77).

Gustav Stresemann, der gewiß bedeutendste Staatsmann der Weimarer Republik, starb im Oktober 1929. Hunderttausende drängten sich am Straßenrand, als der Trauerzug das Brandenburger Tor passierte (79). Mancher mochte das Gefühl gehabt haben, daß hier nicht nur ein großer Staatsmann, sondern die ganze Republik zu Grabe getragen wurde.

Nicht nur als Kulisse staatlicher Repräsentation spielte das Tor eine Rolle, sondern auch als Motiv der bildenden Kunst, die in der Weimarer Republik eine bemerkenswerte Blüte erlebte. Es fällt auf, wie viele Künstler gerade jener Jahre das Brandenburger Tor gemalt haben: Lesser Ury (62), Ernst Ludwig Kirchner (80), Conrad Felixmüller, Oskar Kokoschka (81), Hans Baluschek (82) oder Felix Nussbaum (83), um nur einige zu nennen. Während es Nussbaum, der 1944 in Auschwitz umkam, mit seinem Bild »Der tolle Platz« trotz zerstörtem Liebermann-Palais und zerbrochener Siegessäule nicht um Visionen ging, sondern um die Auseinandersetzung mit dem konservativen Kulturbetrieb der Akademie der Künste, hat Theo Matejko 1933 mit geradezu beängstigender Hellsichtigkeit in einer Kohlezeichnung festgehalten, was sich zwölf Jahre später tatsächlich ereignen sollte: Tod und Zerstörung würden über Berlin kommen, das Brandenburger Tor würde eine Ruine sein (89).

»Im lodernden Schein der Fackeln«

Weltwirtschaftskrise, Massenarbeitslosigkeit, die Unfähigkeit der demokratischen Parteien, die Dinge in den Griff zu bekommen, und das Erstarken radikaler Kräfte auf der linken und rechten Seite des politischen Spektrums versetzten der Weimarer Republik den Todesstoß. Am 30. Januar 1933 zog Hitler in die Reichskanzlei ein. Sein Gauleiter, Joseph Goebbels, hatte zur Feier der »Machtergreifung« einen dreieinhalbstündigen Fackelzug nationalsozialistischer und deutschnationaler Formationen durch das Brandenburger Tor und die Wilhelmstraße inszeniert. »Es ist fast wie ein Traum...«, beschrieb er seine Gefühle. »Wir stehen oben am Fenster, und Hunderttausende und Hunderttausende von Menschen ziehen im lodernden Schein der Fackeln am greisen Reichspräsidenten und jungen Kanzler vorbei und rufen ihnen ihre Dankbarkeit und ihren Jubel zu...« Da die Fotos vom Fackelzug zu dunkel geworden waren, verwendete Goebbels später für Propagandazwecke nachgestellte Aufnahmen aus dem 1933 gedrehten Film »Hans Westmar«, einer NS-Märtyrersaga, die das Leben des SA-Mannes Horst Wessel erzählt (87, 88).

In der Nacht zum 28. Februar 1933 war es nicht der Schein von Fackeln, sondern das brennende Reichstagsgebäude, das den Langhans-Bau in ein gespenstisches Licht tauchte (90). Zwar war der Brandstifter, der 24jährige holländische Kommunist Marinus van der Lubbe, ein Einzeltäter, doch kam der Anschlag den Nationalsozialisten für eine erste große Verhaftungswelle in den Reihen ihrer politischen Gegner gerade recht. Fünftausend Oppositionelle aus dem ganzen Land wurden festgesetzt und verschwanden in Lagern und Gefängnissen. Und mit der Notverordnung »Zum Schutz von Volk und Staat« wurden die wichtigsten Grundrechte der Weimarer Verfassung aus den Angeln gehoben.

Eine Woche später fanden Reichstagswahlen statt, bei denen die Hitler-Partei trotz aller brutalen Einschüchterungen nicht die absolute Mehrheit erzielte. Doch zusammen mit ihren deutschnationalen Koalitionspartnern erreichte sie eine verfassungsmäßige Mehrheit von 51,9 Prozent. Die Eröffnung des neuen Reichstags wurde am 21. März 1933 mit gewaltigem Pomp in Potsdam inszeniert. Am Abend desselben Tages zogen wiederum Zehntausende Nationalsozialisten im Fackelzug durch das Brandenburger Tor (91), das hinfort in immer dichterer Folge den Durchmarsch von NS-Verbänden aller Art erleben sollte (94, 95).

Durch politische Unterdrückung einerseits, durch geschickt inszenierte Massenveranstaltungen und erfolgreiche Arbeitsbeschaffungsmaßnahmen andererseits gelang es den Nationalsozialisten rasch, den Anschein innerer Ruhe und Prosperität zu erwecken. Die für das Jahr 1936 an Berlin vergebenen Olympischen Spiele kamen ihnen für ihre Selbstdarstellungsbemühungen gut zupaß. Die Reichshauptstadt wurde herausgeputzt, und man organisierte ein grandioses Schauspiel, das vom 1. bis zum 16. August einer staunenden Welt präsentiert wurde. Man gab sich weltoffen, friedfertig, als idealer Gastgeber. Die Wirkung nach innen wie nach außen war kolossal, verstärkt durch den erstmaligen systematischen Einsatz von Rundfunkübertragungen in alle Welt.

Im Mittelpunkt stand wieder einmal das Brandenburger Tor, das nicht nur das offizielle Plakat für die Spiele schmückte (98), sondern das selbst mit Olympiafahnen und Girlanden reich behängt war (99–101) und den Besuchermassen den Weg öffnete aus der Stadt hinaus zum herrlich gelegenen Olympiagelände.

Im Zusammenhang mit den fieberhaften Vorbereitungen für die Olympischen Spiele hatte es ein Jahr zuvor, am 20. August 1935, in unmittelbarer Nähe des Brandenburger Tores einen folgenschweren Unfall gegeben. Beim Bau einer unterirdischen Nord-Süd-Verbindung der S-Bahn war es in der damaligen Hermann-Göring-Straße, der heutigen Ebertstraße, infolge ungenügender Sicherheitsmaßnahmen zu einem Einsturz der Baustelle gekommen, der neunzehn Menschenleben forderte (97).

Ein Jahr nach den Olympischen Spielen, im August 1937, gab die 700-Jahrfeier Berlins den Anlaß für einen prachtvollen Festzug, der quer durch die Stadt führte und natürlich das wiederum mit Girlanden geschmückte Brandenburger Tor passierte. Ganz Berlin war auf den Beinen (102, 103). Kaum einer der Schaulustigen wird geahnt haben, daß er Zeuge der letzten großen Veranstaltung zivilen Charakters war, bevor die Stadt in Schutt und Asche versinken würde.

Im September 1937 zog Benito Mussolini, der italienische Duce, durch das Brandenburger Tor in Berlin ein. Der bombastische Empfang – die Straße Unter den Linden war mit aufwendigen Kulissen und Flaggenschmuck zu einer Triumphstraße des deutschen Nationalsozialismus und des italienischen Faschismus umgestaltet worden (105) – zeugte von der Hybris der verbündeten Diktatoren. Wohin der Weg ging, wurde spätestens 1938 deutlich, als man die im Spanischen Bürgerkrieg eingesetzte Legion Condor durch das vormalige Friedenstor ziehen ließ (107) und am 1. Oktober die sogenannte Sudetenbefreiung mit einem imposanten Lichtdom feierte, der über dem Torbau den Nachthimmel erstrahlen ließ (108).

Am 20. April 1939 feierte Hitler seinen fünfzigsten Geburtstag mit einer furchteinflößenden Militärparade auf der Ost-West-Achse, westlich vom Brandenburger Tor (109). In Gedanken hatten er und seine Anhänger die Grenzen des Landes längst überschritten. Sie wollten »Lebensraum« im Osten erobern und ein Weltreich aufbauen, für das Berlin als Hauptstadt zu klein sein würde. Aus der alten Hauptstadt Preußens und des Deutschen Reiches sollte die Welthauptstadt »Germania« werden. Hitlers »Generalbauinspektor für die Reichshauptstadt«, Albert Speer, entwarf gigantische Bauten, die jeden menschlichen Maßstab vermissen ließen (110, 111). Eine neben dem Reichstag geplante 75 Meter hohe »Halle des Volkes« hätte diesen und das Brandenburger Tor städtebaulich zu völliger Bedeutungslosigkeit verurteilt. Doch am 1. September 1939 entfesselte Hitler den Zweiten Weltkrieg, und seine Welthauptstadtpläne blieben Papier.

Polenfeldzug, Frankreichfeldzug: Noch einmal marschierten am 18. Juli 1940 siegreiche Truppen durch das Brandenburger Tor, und die Berliner jubelten ihnen zu – weniger aus Kriegsbegeisterung als aus Erleichterung über die raschen Erfolge (114, 115). Doch dann, 1943, kam der Bombenkrieg nach Berlin, und zum Jubeln war kein Anlaß mehr (118). Stadtviertel um Stadtviertel versank in Schutt und Asche, Tausende verloren ihr Leben.

Mit dem Überfall auf die Sowjetunion und dem Vormarsch deutscher Truppen bis in den Kaukasus war der Bogen endgültig überspannt. Der deutschen Niederlage im Kessel von Stalingrad folgte der unaufhaltsame Vormarsch der Roten Armee. Inzwischen wurden die letzten Ressourcen des Landes mobilisiert. Selbst das Kupferblech der Dacheindeckung des bis dahin noch unzerstörten Brandenburger Tores wurde im Februar 1943 abmontiert, da man es als »kriegswichtiges Material« benötigte.

Als die Rote Armee im Februar 1945 die Oder überschritt, lebten im zerbombten Berlin noch 2,8 Millionen Menschen. Am 16. April 1945 wurde das Signal zur letzten Offensive gegeben: Der Kampf um Berlin begann. Mit 22 000 Geschützen und Hunderten von Kampfflugzeugen wurde der letzte Verteidigungsring der deutschen Wehrmacht um die Reichshauptstadt unter Beschuß genommen. Und zur Mittagszeit des 21. April schlugen die ersten Granaten am Pariser Platz und Unter den Linden ein. Am 30. April stürmten sowjetische Soldaten den Reichstag und hißten auf der Kuppel des ausgebrannten Parlamentsgebäudes die Sowjetflagge. Am selben Tag nahm sich Hitler im Bunker der nahegelegenen Reichskanzlei das Leben. Am 1. Mai wurde auch das zur Panzersperre umfunktionierte, völlig verbarrikadierte Brandenburger Tor (119) von sowjetischen Truppen erstürmt. Über der völlig zerschossenen Quadriga wehte nun ebenfalls die rote Fahne (121–123).

Kalter Krieg

Der Kampf um Berlin war beendet, die deutsche Wehrmacht hatte kapituliert. Vor der gespenstischen Kulisse der völlig zerbombten Stadt und des zerschossenen Brandenburger Tores hielten Einheiten der Roten Armee ihre Siegesparade ab (124, 125). Die einstige Vier-Millionen-Metropole war in einem unübersehbaren Chaos von 75 Millionen Kubikmeter Schutt versunken, einem Siebtel der gesamten Trümmermassen des Deutschen Reiches. Jeder Verkehr war zusammengebrochen, ebenso die Versorgung mit Strom, Gas und Wasser. Es sollte Monate und Jahre dauern, bis das Leben in Berlin wieder in geordneten Bahnen verlaufen konnte.

Im Tiergarten, in unmittelbarer Nähe des Brandenburger Tores, begannen die Sowjets ein Ehrenmal für ihre gefallenen Soldaten zu errichten. Bereits am Jahrestag der Oktoberrevolution, dem 11. November 1945, konnte es eingeweiht werden. Zu diesem Zeitpunkt waren die Sowjets schon nicht mehr die einzigen Sieger, die Berlin besetzt hielten. Am 4. Juli waren britische und amerikanische Truppen in die ihnen zugewiesenen Sektoren eingerückt (127); im August waren französische Einheiten gefolgt.

Der Alltag in Berlin war von Not und Elend geprägt. Die katastrophale Mangelwirtschaft führte zum Aufblühen von Schwarzmärkten, auf denen sich ein schwunghafter Handel zwischen der Berliner Bevölkerung und den Besatzungssoldaten entfaltete. Die Umgebung des Brandenburger Tores war hierfür eine erste Adresse (130). Angesichts der kritischen Ernährungslage rief der von den Sowjets eingesetzte Oberbürgermeister Arthur Werner am 15. Februar 1946 die Berliner Bevölkerung auf, jeden Quadratmeter Boden zum Anbau von Lebensmitteln zu nutzen. Folge war, daß im Frühjahr 1946 der Tiergarten fast vollständig gerodet und in Kleingärten aufgeteilt wurde (134).

Die Landwirtschaft vor dem Brandenburger Tor erwies sich als recht erfolgreich: Beim Erntefest im Herbst 1946 konnte verkündet werden, daß 20 000 Zentner Gemüse und Kartoffeln geerntet worden waren. Man feierte einen fünfzig Pfund schweren Kürbis, einen drei Pfund schweren Wirsingkohl und eine Tomatenpflanze mit 76 Früchten.

Doch die Idylle im Herzen Berlins trog. Rund um die Stadt entwickelte sich das, was als »kalter Krieg« in die Geschichte eingehen sollte. Die gegensätzlichen Interessen der vormals Verbündeten brachen sich Bahn und führten zur unerbittlichen Konfrontation zwischen den drei Westalliierten auf der einen, der Sowjetunion auf der anderen Seite.

Als die drei Westmächte ihre Zonen wirtschaftlich zusammenschlossen und am 20. Juni 1948 eine separate Währungsreform durchführten, versuchte Stalin vier Tage später die Westsektoren Berlins mit einer vollständigen Blockade in die Knie zu zwingen. Elf Monate lang wurde die Halbstadt per Luftbrücke versorgt, dann gaben die Sowjets nach. Doch der Prozeß der Teilung Deutschlands und Berlins schritt weiter voran. Am 24. Mai 1949 trat das Grundgesetz für die Bundesrepublik Deutschland in Kraft, am 7. Oktober desselben Jahres folgte die Gründung der Deutschen Demokratischen Republik. Die Westsektoren Berlins wurden Bundesland, der Ostsektor wurde Hauptstadt der DDR. Das Brandenburger Tor, das Friedenstor, lag plötzlich unmittelbar an einer Grenze. Ein Hinüber und Herüber war zwar noch möglich, doch die beiden Stadthälften entwickelten sich – entsprechend den beiden Staaten und Gesellschaftssystemen, denen sie nun angehörten – immer weiter auseinander. Während der Westen sein Wirtschaftswunder erlebte, ächzte der Osten unter sowjetischen Reparationsforderungen und planwirtschaftlichen Zwängen.

Als die ostdeutsche SED-Regierung am 16. Juni 1953 die ohnehin strengen Arbeitsnormen weiter erhöhte, kam es zu spontanen Arbeitsniederlegungen, die am 17. Juni zu einem Volksaufstand gegen das kommunistische Regime eskalierten. In Berlin erklommen junge Arbeiter das Brandenburger Tor, holten die rote Fahne herunter und verbrannten sie (138–140). Mit schwarz-rot-goldenen Fahnen zogen sie sodann, das Deutschlandlied singend, durch den Langhans-Bau gen Westen (141). Der sowjetische Stadtkommandant verhängte über Ost-Berlin den Ausnahmezustand. Überall in der Stadt fuhren russische Panzer auf, und die »ruhmreiche« Rote Armee schlug im Verein mit DDR-Volkspolizisten den Aufstand nieder. Die traurige Bilanz: mehr als 260 Todesopfer, 21 Demonstranten wurden standrechtlich erschossen, etwa 20 SED-Funktionäre, Volksarmisten und Stasi-Agenten wurden von der aufgebrachten Menge gelyncht, rund 20 000 Menschen wurden in Untersuchungshaft genommen, 3000 von ihnen erhielten zum Teil mehrjährige Haftstrafen.

»Es gibt keine Macht der Erde, die das deutsche Volk auf die Dauer zu einem Sklavenvolk erniedrigen kann«, erklärte der Regierende Bürgermeister von West-Berlin, Ernst Reuter, und fuhr fort: »Wir werden der Welt zeigen, daß es möglich ist, auch mit einem totalitären Regime fertig zu werden, weil wir entschlossen sind, unter allen Umständen unser Ziel zu erreichen. Das Ziel unserer nationalen Einheit, das Ziel unserer Freiheit und das Ziel, das uns allen heilig ist und am Herzen liegt: Frieden für die Welt...« Und die »New York Times« schrieb am 18. Juni: »...wir wissen jetzt, und die Welt weiß es, daß in dem deutschen Volk ein Mut und ein Geist leben, die die Unterdrückung nicht ewig dulden werden.«

Je frostiger der kalte Krieg zwischen Ost und West wurde, desto tiefer wurde die Spaltung Deutschlands und Berlins. Systematisch negierte oder vertuschte man auf östlicher Seite alle Gemeinsamkeiten der Geschichte und beseitigte die Überreste, die daran erinnern mochten. So war bereits 1950 auf ausdrücklichen Befehl von DDR-Staatschef Walter Ulbricht das Berliner Stadtschloß gesprengt worden. Der alte Hohenzollernsitz galt den neuen Machthabern als Symbol alles dessen, was man haßte: Preußentum, Deutschtum. Zwar war das riesige Gebäude durch den Bombenkrieg arg ramponiert, doch hätte man den größten profanen Barockbau nördlich der Alpen durchaus retten können.

Ein ähnliches Schicksal hätte beinahe das Brandenburger Tor ereilt. Zumindest kursierten in den Jahren 1946 und 1947 Gerüchte über die geplante Beseitigung des Langhans-Baus. Doch am 17. November 1949 meldete der »Telegraf am Abend«: »Seit geraumer Zeit fühlt sich jeder gute Berliner von Gerüchten über das Brandenburger Tor beunruhigt. Der unselige Plan, es ganz abzureißen, ist inzwischen endgültig zu den Akten gelegt. Es hat ja auch zum Glück nur wenig gelitten und kann leicht wieder ausgebessert werden. Schlimmer steht es mit der von Schadow geschaffenen Quadriga, dem das Tor krönenden Viergespann. Es ist vom Kriege so schwer beschädigt worden, daß es kaum reparierbar ist. Und es hieß bereits, eben diese Quadriga solle durch ein anderes Monument ersetzt werden.«

Im Mai 1950 wurden die zertrümmerten Reste der Quadriga durch Brigaden der »Freien Deutschen Jugend« (FDJ) entfernt, und das Dach des stark beschädigten, ein Jahr zuvor nur notdürftig gesicherten Brandenburger Tores war erstmals seit Napoleons Zeiten wieder kahl. An der Stelle der Schadow-Gruppe stand nun ein Mast, an dem eine rote Fahne wehte.

Die am Tor vorgenommenen Sicherungsmaßnahmen konnten nur provisorischer Natur sein. Im September 1956 beschloß man in Ost-Berlin, den Langhans-Bau gründlich und auf Dauer instandzusetzen und auch wieder mit einem bekrönenden Schmuck zu versehen. Glücklicherweise ließ man den Gedanken fallen, anstelle der Quadriga ein monumentales Aktivistenpaar aufzurichten. Vielmehr kam es zu dem erstaunlichen Vorgang, daß sich auf dem Höhepunkt des kalten Krieges der damalige Oberbürgermeister von Ost-Berlin, Friedrich Ebert jun., in einem Schreiben an seinen West-Berliner Kollegen wandte und um leihweise Überlassung der Gipsformen des Viergespanns bat. Diese waren gerade noch rechtzeitig vor dem Bombenkrieg vom Original abgenommen worden und lagerten nun in der Gipsformerei der Staatlichen Museen in Berlin-Charlottenburg. Auf einer Pressekonferenz in Ost-Berlin wurde mitgeteilt, die Rekonstruktion des Tores sei Teil eines Plans zur Verschönerung der Hauptstadt der DDR. Mit dem Abschluß der Arbeiten sei bis zum Ende des Jahres 1957 zu rechnen.

Grundsätzlich war man auch auf West-Berliner Seite von dem Rekonstruktionsplan angetan, doch konnte man sich nicht dazu verstehen, die unersätzlichen Gipsformen aus den Händen zu geben. Und so teilte Bürgermeister Franz Amrehn seinem Ost-Berliner Kollegen Ende September 1956 in einem Brief mit, daß man ein Angebot Ernst Reuters aus dem

Jahre 1950 erneuern und die Quadriga auf Kosten des West-Berliner Senats neu herstellen lassen wolle. Sobald das Tor fertiggestellt sei, werde man das neue Viergespann übergeben. Zwar nannte das »Neue Deutschland« diesen Brief eine Unverschämtheit, doch ließen sich beide Stadthälften auf den Handel ein.

Am 14. Dezember 1957 feierten die Ost-Berliner bei unwirtlichem Schneeregen Richtfest. Vor dem noch eingerüsteten Tor hatte man eine girlandengeschmückte Tribüne aufgestellt, von der herab der stellvertretende Ost-Berliner Bürgermeister Waldemar Schmidt die ideologischen Gegner im Westteil der Stadt mit neuen Angriffen bedachte (144, 145). »Hätte der Schöneberger Senat«, so rief er aus, »im vergangenen Jahr uns die Gipsformen leihweise überlassen, so wäre es wahrscheinlich möglich gewesen, heute bereits mit dem Aufstellen der Quadriga zu beginnen. Aber die Frontstadt-Politiker wollten es anders. Die ganze Welt erlebte das beschämende Schauspiel, daß selbst die Wiederherstellung dieses Wahrzeichens unserer Stadt nicht aus dem kalten Krieg ausgeklammert, sondern von ihnen zur Hetze gegen die Arbeiter- und Bauern-Macht benutzt wurde.«

Und der Maurerpolier Tietz setzte mit seinem Richtspruch noch eins drauf: »Am Tag des Richtfestes geloben wir uns, alle Kraft dafür einzusetzen, daß diese Kulturbauten nie wieder einem imperialistischen Krieg zum Opfer fallen. Wir verpflichten uns weiterhin, das Banner der Freiheit, welches die ruhmreiche sowjetische Armee im Mai 1945 als Wahrzeichen des Sieges und des Friedens gehißt hat, zu verteidigen.«

Während man sich auf dem Pariser Platz der propagandistischen Effekthascherei hingab, hatte man in den Werkstätten der im West-Berliner Stadtteil Friedenau gelegenen Bildgießerei Hermann Noack mit zum Teil ganz unerwarteten Problemen zu kämpfen (146–155). Denn man wollte die Quadriga nicht nur originalgetreu nachbauen, sondern zugleich die technischen Mängel, die Ende des 18. Jahrhunderts bei der Fertigung des Originals unterlaufen waren, korrigieren. So führte die vorgenommene Verstärkung der Kupferbleche zu völlig neuen statischen Berechnungen und machte es erforderlich, die fünf Zentimeter starken Eisenstangen, die die alte Quadriga gestützt hatten, durch sieben Zentimeter starke Stahlgerüste zu ersetzen. Im Interesse einer höheren Standfestigkeit war es zudem erforderlich, einigen Pferdebeinen eine leicht veränderte Stellung zu geben. Schließlich mußte zum Schutz vor Witterungseinflüssen die ganze Stahlkonstruktion mit drei Kunstharzüberzügen versehen werden. Durch alle diese Maßnahmen erhöhten sich die Kosten von veranschlagten 150 000 DM auf 250 000 DM.

Endlich, Ende Juli 1958, war die Quadriga fertig (156). Als die Firma Noack sich daranmachte, die Einzelteile mit Kranwagen und Tiefladern zum Brandenburger Tor zu bringen und die Montage vorzubereiten, verboten die Ost-Berliner Behörden die Aufstellung der Gruppe durch den westlichen Hersteller. So mußte man sich darauf beschränken, die monumentalen Pferde samt der Siegesgöttin und ihrem Wagen durch das Tor hindurch von West nach Ost zu expedieren und auf dem Pariser Platz abzuladen (157, 158). Sofort fanden sich einige hundert Schaulustige ein, die das alte Berliner Freiheits- und Friedenssymbol freudig begrüßten. Und sogar Oberbürgermeister Friedrich Ebert jun. erschien, um sich vor dem kupfernen Viergespann ablichten zu lassen. Rechtzeitig vor seinem Eintreffen jedoch waren die Trophäen der Siegesgöttin, das Eiserne Kreuz und der Adler, die beiden alten preußischen Symbole, die seit der Wiederaufstellung der Quadriga im Jahre 1814 integraler Bestandteil des Standbildes gewesen waren, mit einem Sack verhüllt worden (160).

Das alles geschah am Freitag, dem 1. August 1958. Am Montag, dem 4. August, schlug es wie eine Bombe ein: Die »BZ« machte ihre Titelseite mit der Überschrift auf: »Die Quadriga gestohlen! Nachts in Ostberlin fortgeschafft.« Wohin man die Göttin und ihr Viergespann verbracht hatte, war einer im besten Amtsdeutsch abgefaßten Presseerklärung des Senats von West-Berlin zu entnehmen: »Die bisher noch immer nicht einleuchtend erklärte Verbringung der Quadriga in den Marstall ist... ein offener, von östlicher Seite auch nicht bestrittener Bruch der zwischen den Beauftragten getroffenen Vereinbarungen und in jedem Falle rechtswidrig. Noch vor der Anlieferung ist das Verlangen nach einer förmlichen Verwaltungsübergabe zur freien Verfügung über das Werk abgelehnt und daraufhin die Übergabeverhandlung nicht mehr zur Voraussetzung der Inbetriebnahme gemacht worden. Hiernach haben die Stellen im Ostsektor lediglich das Recht zur unverzüglichen Aufstellung der Quadriga auf dem Tor. Jede andere Verwendung oder Verbringung bedeutet daher auch eine Rechtsverletzung. Eine Aufklärung der tatsächlichen Motive über das Verhalten der Stellen im Ostsektor ist bis zur Stunde nicht möglich gewesen.«

Der Grund für die vorübergehende Unterbringung des Standbildes auf dem Hof des alten Marstalls (161) war folgender: Das SED-Regime wollte sich mit dem Preußen-Adler und dem Eisernen Kreuz nicht abfinden und hatte diese »Symbole des preußischen, deutschen Militarismus« in einer Nacht- und Nebelaktion entfernen lassen. Vorschläge für einen eventuellen Ersatz: anstelle des Adlers eine Friedenstaube oder gar den Sowjetstern; anstelle des Eisernen Kreuzes einen fünfzackigen Stern, Hammer und Sichel oder das DDR-Emblem Hammer und Zirkel (159). Nichts von alledem fand Zustimmung, und so kam es zu jenem Provisorium, das bis zur vorerst letzten Abnahme der Quadriga im Frühjahr 1990 bestand: Adler und Kreuz wurden abmontiert und im Märkischen Museum deponiert. Die Panierstange in der Hand der Viktoria schmückte fortan nur der leere Eichenkranz.

Dennoch freute sich Berlin, als es am 28. September 1958 die Aufstellung der Quadriga feiern konnte, die nun, wie man hoffte, ruhigeren Zeiten entgegenfahren würde (162, 163). Und in der Tat schien es, zumindest um das Brandenburger Tor herum, ruhiger und normaler zu werden. Staatsbesuche stellten sich wie ehedem ein und schauten hinüber und herüber, unterm Lichterbaum sangen die Schöneberger Sängerknaben zu Füßen der Quadriga Weihnachtslieder, sowjetische Soldaten nahmen zum Fototermin Aufstellung vor der Torkulisse und US-Regisseur Billy Wilder drehte hier sogar einen Film (164—167). Titel: »Eins, zwei, drei«. Hauptdarsteller: James Cagney, Liselotte Pulver, Horst Buchholz und Hanns Lothar. Thema: eine Parodie auf Ost und West und Coca Cola. Aufgrund der heiklen politischen Situation konnte das Brandenburger Tor allerdings nicht in allen Szenen im Original mitspielen. Wilder hatte gar nicht erst versucht, mit den Ost-Berliner Behörden wegen einer Dreherlaubnis zu verhandeln. Und so war zum damals horrenden Preis von einer Million Mark und unter Verwendung von gewaltigen Mengen Holz, Gips, Farbe und Zement in Münchens Filmstadt Geiselgasteig eine Kopie des Tores, des Pariser Platzes und der »Linden« errichtet worden. Am 13. August 1961 berichtete die »Berliner Morgenpost« über die Dreharbeiten: »Gegen den Regen kann sich ein Mann wie Billy Wilder wehren: Er ließ seine ›Linden‹ mit erheblichen Kosten kanalisieren und asphaltieren — somit machte er die Massenszenen einigermaßen wetterfest. Einem politischen Tief gegenüber ist auch ein Hollywood-Regisseur machtlos. Aber Billy Wilder ist wohl Optimist. Denn gestern kam er nochmals mit seinem Aufnahmestab nach Berlin, um morgen und Dienstag Außenaufnahmen zu drehen.« Doch dazu sollte es nicht mehr kommen...

Die Mauer

An jenem Sonntag, dem 13. August 1961, begann das DDR-Regime, quer durch Berlin eine Mauer zu ziehen. Ost- und Westteil sollten hermetisch voneinander abgeriegelt werden. Noch wenige Wochen zuvor hatte Walter Ulbricht getönt: »Niemand hat die Absicht, eine Mauer zu errichten.« Doch zu diesem Zeitpunkt liefen unter der Regie von Erich Honecker die Vorbereitungen dazu längst auf Hochtouren. Zweck dieser Gewaltmaßnahme, die zugleich die Ohnmacht wie den brutalen Charakter des SED-Regimes offenbarte, war es, die eigenen Bürger an der Flucht in den Westen und damit ein Ausbluten der DDR zu verhindern. Zwischen 1949 und 1961 hatten etwa drei Millionen Menschen das Gebiet der DDR verlassen, und gerade 1961 erhöhte sich die Zahl der Flüchtlinge wieder dramatisch.

In den frühen Morgenstunden jenes Augustsonntags wurden alle Verbindungsstraßen nach West-Berlin entlang der Grenzlinien aufgerissen, Betonpfähle eingerammt, Stacheldraht ausgerollt. Am Brandenburger Tor marschierten Hundertschaften uniformierter »Betriebskampfgruppen« mit gepanzerten Fahrzeugen auf (168–172). Zug um Zug wurden in den folgenden Tagen und Wochen die provisorischen Sperranlagen durch eine feste Mauer ersetzt.

Beispiellose Szenen spielten sich in jenen Tagen ab: Verzweifelte Menschen versuchten, den Stacheldraht zu überwinden. Andere sprangen aus den Fenstern von Häusern, die über Nacht auf einer Grenze standen und deren Zugänge nach Westen versperrt worden waren. DDR-Posten bewachten mit vorgehaltener Waffe die Bauarbeiter, die sich selbst einmauern mußten. Auf der West- wie der Ostseite der Sperranlagen standen Angehörige zerrissener Familien, die sich mit Tränen in den Augen zuwinkten, sowie Tausende von Schaulustigen, denen die Ratlosigkeit ins Gesicht geschrieben stand (179). Ratlos waren auch die Politiker und Militärs, die am 13. August und in den Folgetagen zum Brandenburger Tor und an andere Grenzstellen kamen, allen voran der Regierende Bürgermeister Willy Brandt, der eine Wahlkampfreise in der Bundesrepublik unterbrach und, in den Morgenstunden jenes Unglückssonntags nach Berlin zurückgekehrt, sich sogleich zum Brandenburger Tor begab (176–178).

Den historischen Tagen deutscher Geschichte, an denen das Brandenburger Tor im Brennpunkt stand, hatte sich ein weiterer hinzugesellt – einer der schwärzesten. Zum erstenmal seit seinem Bestehen war der Langhans-Bau kein Stadttor mehr, sondern ein unzugängliches Gebäude im Niemandsland zwischen Ost und West. »Macht das Tor auf« wurde in der Folgezeit immer dort zur Parole, wo Menschen sich versammelten, um die deutsche Einheit einzufordern. Wie sehr der Torbau zum Symbol der deutschen Geschichte geworden war, kam nirgends so prägnant zum Ausdruck wie in dem Satz Richard v. Weizsäckers aus der Zeit, als er Regierender Bürgermeister von West-Berlin war: »Die Deutsche Frage bleibt so lange offen, wie das Brandenburger Tor geschlossen ist.«

In den bitteren Jahren der Spaltung bekam Berlin viele Zeichen der Freundschaft. Menschen aus aller Welt kamen zu Besuch, gingen zur Mauer und äußerten Erschütterung über das, was sie dort zu sehen bekamen. Besonders wichtig für die Stadt und ihren Überlebenswillen war der Besuch John F. Kennedys, der im Juni 1963 an die Spree kam und mit den Worten »Ich bin ein Berliner« der Bevölkerung der Halbstadt seine Solidarität bekundete. Als er das Brandenburger Tor besuchte, hatte das DDR-Regime die Durchfahrten verhängt, um ihm den Blick auf die »Linden« zu verwehren (182).

Während es in den folgenden Jahren, etwa zu Weihnachten 1963, in zähen Verhandlungen zwischen West-Senat und Ost-Magistrat zu sogenannten Passierscheinabkommen kam, die den West-Berlinern Verwandtenbesuche im Ostteil der Stadt erlaubten, wurden die Grenzanlagen immer weiter perfektioniert. Als sie im Juli 1966 auch im Bereich des Brandenburger Tores die Mauer verstärkten und erhöhten, stellten die Ost-Berliner Behörden dort folgendes Schild auf: »Wer die Staatsgrenze mit Gewalt einrennen will, wer an der Mauer provoziert, macht alles nur schlimmer!« (184). Hier erübrigt sich jeder Kommentar.

Die Stadt richtete sich ein und lernte mit der Mauer zu leben. Der Chor derjenigen, die noch »Macht das Tor auf« zu rufen wagten, wurde kleiner und leiser. Im Verlauf der siebziger Jahre kam es zum Vier-Mächte-Abkommen über Berlin, zu einem Abkommen zwischen der Bundesrepublik und der DDR über den Transitverkehr von und nach Berlin sowie zu einer zwischen dem West-Berliner Senat und der DDR-Regierung ausgehandelten Besuchsregelung für West-Berliner. Während an der Ostseite der Mauer weiterhin scharf geschossen wurde — mindestens 73 Menschen verloren hier bei Fluchtversuchen ihr Leben —, verkam die Westseite mehr und mehr zur bloßen Touristenattraktion, vor allem aber zur größten »Leinwand« der Welt, auf der sich Künstler und solche, die sich dafür hielten, austoben konnten. Immer mehr gehörte die Mauer zum Berliner Alltag, immer seltener kam es zu Demonstrationen gegen dieses menschenverachtende Bauwerk (187–190).

So war es ein politisches Ereignis von höchstem Seltenheitswert, als der Präsident der Vereinigten Staaten von Amerika, Ronald Reagan, im Rahmen der 750-Jahrfeier Berlins am 12. Juni 1987 direkt vor dem Brandenburger Tor vor 25 000 Berlinern an Michail Gorbatschow gerichtet ausrief: »Herr Generalsekretär, wenn Sie Frieden suchen, wenn Sie Wohlstand für die Sowjetunion und Osteuropa wünschen, wenn Sie eine Liberalisierung wollen, dann kommen Sie hier zu diesem Tor. Herr Gorbatschow, öffnen Sie dieses Tor! Herr Gorbatschow, reißen Sie diese Mauer nieder!« (192). Gewiß, man war Reagan dankbar für seine Worte, für seinen guten Willen und seinen Optimismus. Aber wer in Deutschland und besonders in Berlin teilte diesen Optimismus noch? Wer ehrlich ist, wird sich wohl eingestehen müssen, nie und nimmer damit gerechnet zu haben, daß die Mauer nur knappe zweieinhalb Jahre nach dieser historischen Rede tatsächlich fallen würde.

»Wir sind ein Volk!«

Am 9. November 1989 war es soweit: Das durch neuerliche Fluchtwellen und gewaltige Massendemonstrationen zermürbte, ohnehin marode SED-Regime brach zusammen. Es öffnete die Grenzen, und die freiheitshungrigen DDR-Bewohner strömten in den Westen. Berlin erlebte einige der glücklichsten Stunden und Tage seiner Geschichte. Ausgelassene Menschen aus Ost und West tanzten auf der Mauer vor dem Brandenburger Tor (193–195). Gerade hier sollte die Mauer nun fallen, gerade hier wollte man die neue Freiheit feiern. Zu lange schon war das Tor Symbol des geteilten Deutschlands gewesen, nun sollte es die wiedergewonnene Einheit symbolisieren. Fernseh- und Rundfunkanstalten aus aller Welt schlugen auf der Straße des 17. Juni, westlich des Torbaus, wochenlang ihr Quartier auf, um bei der Wiedereröffnung des Brandenburger Tores live dabeizusein. Allabendlich versammelten sich Tausende von Berlinern und skandierten den alten Ruf: »Macht das Tor auf!« (198, 199).

Am 22. Dezember 1989, zwei Tage vor Heiligabend, hatte das Warten ein Ende: Bundeskanzler Helmut Kohl, DDR-Ministerpräsident Hans Modrow sowie die Bürgermeister der beiden Stadthälften, Walter Momper und Erhard Krack, eröffneten an diesem geschichts- und symbolträchtigsten Ort Deutschlands einen neuen Übergang durch die bereits löchrig gewordene Mauer (200, 201). In seiner Rede auf dem Pariser Platz sagte Momper: »Die Öffnung des Brandenburger Tores berührt uns in Berlin wie keine andere Grenzöffnung in den vergangenen Wochen davor. An diesem Bauwerk, an diesem Platz hängt unser Herz. Wenn wir Berlinerinnen und Berliner von heute an wieder von beiden Seiten durch das Tor gehen können, dann wissen wir ganz sicher, das Leben wird wieder normal in Berlin. Das Leben wird noch schöner in Berlin.« Und er schloß mit den Worten: »Berlin, nun freue dich!«

In der Nacht vom 31. Dezember 1989 zum 1. Januar 1990 versammelten sich rund um das Brandenburger Tor fast eine halbe Million Menschen zur größten Silvesterfeier, die die Stadt und das Land je erlebt hatten (202, 203). Besser konnten die Berliner nicht unter Beweis stellen, daß sie sich auch nach 28 Jahren erzwungener Trennung nicht fremd geworden waren. Doch als man am frühen Morgen des Neujahrstages daranging, den Pariser Platz und die Umgebung des Tores aufzuräumen, stellte sich Katerstimmung ein. Nicht nur war ein Menschenleben zu beklagen und hatte der Einsturz einer neben dem Torgebäude aufgebauten Videowand zahlreiche Verletzte gefordert, auch war das Tor selbst von dem ausgelassenen Treiben arg in Mitleidenschaft gezogen worden. Seine Wände und Säulen waren übersät mit Graffiti. Und von Rowdys, die zu mitternächtlicher Stunde das Dach des Tores erklommen hatten, waren nicht nur Feuerwerkskörper gezündet, sondern auch Kupferplatten aus der Dachabdeckung herausgerissen und verbogen worden. Vor allem aber hatte die Quadriga unter der Silvester-Invasion gelitten: Der Friedensgöttin hatte man den Lorbeerkranz vom Kopf gerissen und den linken Arm abzutrennen versucht, die Pferde waren mit Fußtritten traktiert worden, das Geschirr durch Kletterer ramponiert.

Bereits am 18. Januar 1990 wurde mit ersten Reparaturen begonnen, doch rasch stellte sich heraus, daß die gesamte Anlage einer intensiven Überholung bedurfte. Und so wurde im März das Tor einmal mehr eingerüstet und das Viergespann zum Zwecke der Restaurierung ins Kreuzberger Museum für Verkehr und Technik gebracht (205–207). In neugewonnener Einmütigkeit arbeiten Ost und West gemeinsam daran, dieses herrliche Bauwerk rechtzeitig zu seinem zweihundertsten Geburtstag am 6. August 1991 in neuem Glanz und alter Pracht wiederherzustellen. Es wird der erste Festtag sein, an dem das Tor nicht Kulisse ist, sondern selbst gefeiert wird. Und auch dann wird es wieder sein, was es stets gewesen ist: Brennpunkt deutscher Geschichte.

Carl Gotthard Langhans, 1732–1808, Künstler unbekannt / Unknown artist

Johann Gottfried Schadow,
1764–1850, Kupferstich
von A. Wolf nach einer
Zeichnung von F. Krüger.
Copper engraving by
A. Wolf, based on a drawing
by F. Krüger

Preface

Two dates have served as inspiration for this book: The 6th of August 1991, and the 22nd of December 1989. The first commemorates the 200th anniversary of the Brandenburg Gate and stands for the eventful history of this building. The second date marks the reopening of the Gate after it had been blocked by the Berlin Wall for twenty-eight years and stands for the symbolism inherent in this masterpiece by the famous architect Langhans.

In the course of its twohundred-year existence the Brandenburg Gate has been the focus of German history more often than any other edifice in Germany. From Napoleon's entrance into Berlin in 1806 to the victory parades after Bismarck's wars for German unification, the November revolution of 1918, Hitler's seizing of power on 30th January 1933, the Capitulation on 8th May 1945, the people's revolt in the GDR on 17th June 1953, the erection of the Wall on 13th August 1961 and, finally, to the collapse of the GDR-Regime on 9th November 1989: The Gate always served as the scene of action or as the backdrop for magnificent festivities and parades or, again, for manifestations of political or military defeat. The numerous, often dramatic events hiding behind the two dates mentioned, of which the Brandenburg Gate was a witness, have turned this building into a unique symbol of German history.

There are other structures symbolising German history, such as the Cathedral at Aix-la-Chapelle, the Wartburg Castle, Paul's Church at Frankfurt, the Cathedral at Cologne and also the Reichstag (Parliament Building) at Berlin. But they all stand for limited historic epochs or certain spiritual currents. Other monuments which were intended to serve as national symbols, such as the Memorial to the Battle of the Nations at Leipzig, the Memorial of Hermann's Victory over the Romans in the Teutoburg Forest, the Walhalla, the Niederwald-Memorial to the war of 1870/71 or the Kaiser-Wilhelm-National-Monument on the Kyffhäuser Mountain. All of them today are reduced to mere tourist sights.

Precisely because it was not originally conceived as a national shrine and also because it does reflect the highs as well as the lows of German history, the Brandenburg Gate became a national symbol and as such has always been convincing and uncontested. How it grew into this role the present volume sets out to document.

"Taking the Athens Town-Gate for a Model"

When preparations were begun, in the early summer of 1788, to tear down the old Brandenburg Gate separating the Berlin Dorotheenstadt area from Tiergarten Park, the Gate had stood for only about fifty-four years. It had been built in 1734 under King Friedrich Wilhelm I, as an unadorned structure in the baroque style. We know what it looked like from an engraving dated 1764: Two baroque gate posts, enhanced by pilasters and trophies, the passages on both sides decorated with vases (1, 2)*. At night, wooden doors closed off the gateways, but during the daytime there was lively traffic to and from Berlin.

In 1786, Friedrich Nicolai, the Berlin chronicler, noted down the following description of the surroundings: "At right, towards the Spree River and next to the Brandenburg Gate lies the big parade ground. Along the near side of it, an avenue — called the avenue of the Prince-Electors — leads to a large square bordering the Spree... On the side running along the banks of the Spree, tents and booths are set up in the summer where various kinds of refreshments are sold... On fine days, especially on Sundays and Holidays, at about 6 o'clock in the afternoon, thousands of people gather here for a promenade on foot, on horseback or in carriages — while by order of the commandant, musicians of the infantry and artillery regiments garrisoned in Berlin are dissimulated in the adjacent bushes, the whole making for a charming spectacle..."

On both sides of the Gate, smaller buildings of a rather plain aspect were grouped. Seen from the city, the guard house was situated on the left, whereas on the right there was a house for the customs inspector as well as a fire-station. And since 1767, also on the right-hand side, stood the barracks for the Herzog-Friedrich-Infantry-Regiment. Altogether by no means an unsightly complex of buildings. And yet there was criticism, for example in a 1776 publication entitled "Kritische Anmerkungen über den Zustand der Baukunst in Berlin und Potsdam" "Critical Remarks Concerning the State of Architecture in Berlin and Potsdam", where it says: "The Brandenburg Gate in particular, considering its prominent location, would well be deserving of an improvement in its exterior."

King Friedrich Wilhelm II of Prussia seems to have been of the same opinion. And so it was probably he who entrusted Carl Gotthard Langhans with the design for a new town gate. Langhans promptly presented his King with a memorandum in which he explains: "The situation of the Brandenburg Gate being, in its way, uncontestably the most beautiful in the world, and in order to take the most advantage of this by giving the Gate the greatest possible opening, I have, for the construction of a new Gate, thought of taking the Athens town gate for a model..."

Who was the man, who is here outlining to his King the plans for what was to become one of Berlin's finest buildings? Carl Gotthard Langhans was born on 15th December 1732 in Landeshut/Silesia. He died in 1808 in Grüneiche near Breslau. While studying architecture, he travelled extensively in Italy, Holland, England and France. After being named Oberbaurat (Chief Building Counsellor) in 1775, he worked almost exclusively in Silesia, his province of origin, until, in 1786, he received a call to Berlin where eventually he became director of the Oberhofbauamt (The Court's Building Office). It was Langhans who designed such important buildings as the Belvedere in the park of the Charlottenburg Palace or the Marble Palais in Potsdam. But he was also in charge of the restoration, executed in neo-gothic

---

* Bracketed numbers within the text refer to illustrations.

style, of the spires of St. Mary's Church in Berlin. He even extended his work to interior design when he created the staircase and the so-called 'Seashell Room' for Rheinsberg Chateau and the banquet hall for Bellevue Palace in Berlin. Foremost among his theatre buildings is the first German National Theatre which stood on Gendarmenmarkt in Berlin until it burned down in 1817. Today, however, the name Langhans is associated primarily with his masterpiece, the Brandenburg Gate.

Langhans' remark in his memorandum to the King according to which he had taken the Propylaea at Athens, i.e. the gateway to the Acropolis, as a model, occasioned Johann Gottfried Schadow in his book "Kunstwerke und Kunstansichten" (Works of Art and Views on Art) to ridicule his colleague: "Did he distrust his own ideas or was it laziness? Suffice it to say that he liked to borrow. He had filled his sketch books while travelling, and a remake of acknowledged masterworks appeared to him safer than new original designs from any one of us." A hundred years later, one could still read about Langhans in a "History of Berlin Architecture": "Without any originality and working at a time when taste was at a nadir, he was yet able to follow noble patterns."

All this sounds rather unfavourable and disregards the fact that Langhans quite intentionally followed Johann Joachim Winckelmann's enthusiasm for classical Greek architecture, the latter having proclaimed Hellenic art as intrinsically creative, as truly the art of the classical period.

A model of the Langhans Gate was shown on 16th August 1789 in Berlin on the occasion of a public assembly of the Academy of Fine Arts held in honour of the King's sister, Friederike Wilhelmine von Oranien-Nassau. And from the 25th September of the same year, visitors to a public exhibition of art, organised by the Academy, were able to admire the model. Contrasting with medieval town gates whose task it was to serve as a bastion against enemies from without, the generous architectural design of the new Brandenburg Gate expressed the cosmopolitanism of a self-assured capital.

According to various estimates, the construction of the Gate (3), which was started in 1789, probably cost upwards of five hundred thousand thalers. Hundreds of thousands of bricks as well as great numbers of field- and limestones were needed. Saxony sandstone came by water from Cotta, Pirna and Postelwitz. 1240 sq.ft. of sheet iron were used, 991 cartloads of sand had to be provided and 389 cartloads of rubble were removed from the site.

The Court had charged Minister von Woellner with supervision of the construction which, by order of the King, had to be speeded up several times. But although pressed for time, Langhans himself looked after every little detail. Thus he wrote to one of the suppliers, a merchant named Funicke, on 26 August 1798: "I would not be adverse to employing so-called 'ketter-stone' for the centre cornice, providing same is of the white kind which does not erode." For the protection of the stone carvers' work, generous coatings using putty, oil and paint were foreseen. But since the sum of 1.599 thalers estimated for this work seemed too high to Minister von Woellner, he stipulated that the sandstones should be joined with a lower grade of putty and coated with simple whitewash which would bring down the cost to a mere 1.279 thalers.

The Gate had not yet been provided with all its sculptural ornaments when, after a construction period of two years, it was unceremoniously opened to traffic (4, 5). A protocol established on the occasion runs as follows: "Actum, Berlin 6th August 1791. When by order of His Royal Majesty the passageway of the newly erected Brandenburg Gate was opened today, the military detachment charged with mounting guard at this Gate, moved into the newly built guard house..." Neither was the old Prussian Royal hymn intoned on the occasion, as at one time was presumed, nor did the King attend the opening — he was in Pillnitz trying to work out a pact with Emperor Leopold II.

There it stood now, the Brandenburg Gate, and has been standing ever since. With a width of 65,5 metres, a depth of 11 metres and a height, including the Quadriga, of ca. 26 metres, along with its dynamic yet clear design it separates the boulevard "Unter den Linden" and the square "Pariser Platz" from the Tiergarten Park. The monumental complex, flanked by two wing buildings, consists of five gateways which are separated from one another by massive transverse walls. The façades of these walls are adorned with doric-style sandstone pillars — six on either side of the Gate. While the four outer gateways have a width of 3.79 metres each, the centre passage is 5.50 metres wide. It was reserved for the exclusive use of the members of the Court. A doric entablature and an attic rest upon the pillars on which, with a socle for additional prominence, the Quadriga was later to be mounted.

The sculptural work, executed in sandstone by artisans from Berlin and Potsdam, is based largely on designs by Johann Gottfried Schadow. Thus the 32 small reliefs in the entablature of the two longitudinal sides of the Gate are attributed to him. Taking up the metopes of the Parthenon in Athens, they depict battle scenes between Lapiths and Centaurs. The bas-relief in the centre of the attic facing towards the city shows a procession of the Goddess of Peace executed after a design by Christian Bernhard Rodes modified somewhat by Schadow (14). Berlin city historian Bogdan Krieger describes this relief as follows: "The Goddess of Peace, holding an olive branch and a laurel wreath in her hands, sits on a triumphal chariot drawn by four putti. Walking in front of the chariot are Harmony, Friendship, Statesmanship, the Goddess of Victory, as well as Courage before which Discord is taking flight. Following the chariot are Joy, dancing and holding a garland of roses in her hands; further the Goddess of Abundance... as well as the arts of Architecture, of Painting, of Sculpturing, and the Goddess of the Sciences along with Music and Poetry."

Mounted on the inside walls of the gateways are twenty reliefs showing scenes from the Heracles legend, of which reproductions are shown in this book (6–11). The bas-relief with the procession of the Goddess of Peace, the metope reliefs and the scenes from the Heracles legend symbolise the hope for an era of peace after a bellicose period, as do the statues of Mars sheathing his sword, and of Minerva (12, 13). Both had originally been placed in niches facing towards the city, between the Gate and its wing buildings. In 1868, when the Brandenburg Gate was rebuilt, they were removed to their present locations, on the side-walls of the building.

Neither these adornments nor the Quadriga were yet in place when on 22nd December 1792, the first ceremonious procession was led through the new Gate: Crown Princess Luise and her sister, Friederike, brides of the King's two eldest sons, were given a festive welcome to Berlin. Two years later, Luise wrote to her brother Georg: "Do you remember that day's festivities, how anxious my heart beat as I approached the gates of Berlin and received all those testimonies of joy and respect... Yes, dearest friend, it was a joyful moment for me when I became a citizen of Berlin."

The Quadriga

As a crowning piece for the Gate, Johann Gottfried Schadow in 1789 designed the Quadriga which, according to the original plans by Langhans, was to represent 'The Triumph of Peace' (15, 16). Schadow was born on 20th May 1764 in Berlin, where he also died on 27th January 1850. There, at the Königliche Werkstatt (Royal Workshop), he studied the art of sculpting with Tassaert until 1785, while at the same time attending the Academy of Art. After a journey to Italy with a prolonged stay at Rome, he returned to Berlin in 1787, where he joined the Königliche Porzellanmanufaktur (Royal China Manufacture) and, after Tassaert's death in 1788, was appointed head of the Hofbildhauerwerkstatt (The Court's Stone Carvers' Workshop). This post also encompassed the prestigious position of 'Director of All Sculptures' at the Oberhofbauamt (The Court's Building Office) headed by Langhans. In 1815, he became Director of the Berlin Academy of Fine Arts.

Around 1800, Schadow is considered the most important German sculptor. Among his nearly threehundred sculptures are such renowned works as the tomb of Graf von der Mark, the marble statue of Friedrich II at Stettin, as well as the famous 'Princesses' Group' — the first life-size twin statue of the classicist period, which represents the sisters Luise and Friederike von Mecklenburg-Strelitz.

Execution of the Quadriga was entrusted to Potsdam coppersmith Emanuel Jury. On 13th March 1789, Langhans, Schadow and Jury met in conference and, according to the record, among other things also discussed the following: "After coppersmith Jury had explained at great length in which manner he intends to untertake this task, it was decided that Mr. Schadow is to construct a model clearly showing the measurements of a group of 4 horses, a chariot and a victoria, after which the large-size model, whose horses should measure 10 feet from ground to head will be fashioned out of wood and at the size the complete group is to have in natura, and which is to serve as the true model... Though Mr. Jury on the whole does not foresee any difficulty in this matter, he demands that he be supplied with either English copper or, if this be refused, the best local copper... As regards gilding, there is at present nobody he could propose..."

The Wohlers, father and son, in Potsdam were charged with the building of the two wooden models. The gilding never came about. Although the catalogue of the 1793 Art Exhibition mentions in regard to the model of the Quadriga a gilding of the Goddess of Victory "with truly genuine gold", King Friedrich Wilhelm II issued the following order on 11th July 1793 to Minister von Woellner: "I... therefore wish that this extraordinarily well turned out Quadriga not be gilt but that she should keep her natural colour. Friedrich Wilhelm."

But we are rushing ahead of events. Schadow started off his design with the horses, to which he gave special attention. To allow him a close study of the movements of the animals, a riding-master of the Royal Stables was ordered to parade on horseback before him so that he could make all the drawings he required. Apparently, however, Schadow did not go to similar length when he designed the Goddess of Victory: According to his own testimony, he only executed one single sketch (17, 18).

Execution of the Quadriga took longer than expected. Several times, Minister von Woellner had to push for continuation of the work. He even had woodcarver Wohler and coppersmith Jury interrogated by authorities. In a written deposition, the woodcarvers stated the following reasons for the delay: "Why we did not sufficiently advance after our accord of 6th May 1789 is due to the fact that, while the measurements of the horses were set at 10 feet on 19th June '89, we received order from Geheimrat (Privy Counsellor) Langhans to stop work as doubts had arisen, and to wait until the Academy of Arts would have determined the proportions of the group. On 15th September '89 we received order to the effect that the Academy had resolved a height of 12 feet for the group... we finished one horse regardless of the fact that everything would have to be enlarged now."

Thus the entire work had to be increased by two feet over what had originally been planned and already partly been executed. In his written justification, coppersmith Emanuel Jury also pointed to this alteration in scale and begged to bear in mind that "such colossuses only come up once in a century and, because of their size, cannot be properly judged and estimated." He proposes to place part of the work into the hands of another coppersmith. This proposal is accepted by his patrons, and execution of the Victoria is transferred to tinsmith Köhler of Potsdam.

At last, in the early summer of 1793, all was ready. On 15th June, Jury reported that the Quadriga would be shipped to Berlin by water the following Monday and would arrive there on Wednesday evening or Thursday morning. The group had hardly reached Berlin when there was official complaint about the nudity of the Victoria. So a mantle had to be quickly forged for her which, when it was attached, necessitated amputation of the goddess' legs.

In his report of 13th September 1793 to von Woellner, Langhans was able to state that the Gate was now approaching completion. The Quadriga would soon be in place, and the coppersmiths were now busy with the restoration of the copper roofing. The area in front of the Gate had been levelled and would be paved. Schadow also made suggestions regarding lighting of the square. Von Woellner wrote on the margin of this report: "Praise God! At last we have gotten that far!"

All that remained to be done now was to provide a means for closing the Gate at night. For the centre passage — the one reserved for the Court — a wooden portal was built which was locked at night. For the gateways on the sides, there were wooden doors for the night and wrought iron gates which generally were also closed during the daytime but did not block out the view towards Tiergarten Park. In the ensuing years, the wooden as well as the iron gates turned out to be continuous sources for trouble. As early as 1795, repairs had to be effected. That year also witnessed the first mishap when a strong wind blew a wing of the main portal shut just after the King had passed through. But things got even worse. On 4th November 1804, the commandant in charge made the following report: "Last night, when the Princess Ferdinand von Preußen [rather the consort of Prince August Ferdinand] passed through the Gate, the storm ripped one of the wings of the portal from a guard and hurled it against the carriage so that the carriage was partly smashed and worse disaster was to be feared. This has occurred several times before and at the other gates as well, whenever there was a strong wind, and has happened twice to Prince August Ferdinand, as the wings of the doors are so big and heavy, and the guard, who has one hand occupied by his musket, thus does not have enough strength to offer sufficient restistance to the storm. The Bauamt (Building Office) is requested to search for a means to remedy this unsatisfactory situation, especially in view of the fact that such high and heavy doors are not really required." But several decades were to pass before the portals were finally removed. For the guards posted at the Gate, duty truly was not easy. Adelbert von Chamisso, poet and explorer, found that out the hard way. A report from the commandant's office of 8th December 1804 states: "As the guard at the Brandenburg Gate was not in proper order and did not execute the salute properly when the King passed through, Lieutenant von Chamisso will be placed under arrest and reported to his regiment..." Years later, danseuse Lola Montez noted in her memoirs: "On Sundays, the guards at the Brandenburg Gate are truly much put upon. Not a minute goes by without their being obliged to salute the equipage of a prince or nobleman."

In 1804, the first thorough renovation of the Brandenburg Gate became necessary. At a cost of 6.500 thalers, the structure had to be cleaned, newly luted, oiled and painted, whereby the new colour in particular occasioned criticism. Thus Julius von Voß, officer and journalist, wrote in 1811 in his publication "The New Berlin": "The architects cannot take credit for the Brandenburg Gate as it is a copy; however, their taste has manifested itself on the structure insofar as, in place of the white colour, suggestive of marble and offering an ideal contrast to the green of the Tiergarten trees, they have soiled it with a revolting café-au-lait colour which does not even bear resemblance to any ordinary kind of stone and thus infringes on the dignity of the entrance to Europe's most beautiful avenue." A most deplorable state of affairs which fortunately was remedied in the years to follow.

Napoleon, the Horse Thief

"Let us pause here and contemplate the Brandenburg Gate and the Victoria upon it. No doubt, after the latest historic events, the goddess is familiar to you. The good woman certainly has had her vicissitudes. She does not show it though, the way she gallantly leads that chariot." When Heinrich Heine wrote this in 1822, the Victoria had indeed been through a good deal. The first blow she suffered was inflicted on her by an emperor: Napoleon. Bonaparte had already spread war all over Europe when, in a twin battle at Jena and Auerstedt on 14th October 1806, he also defeated the Prussian armies of King Friedrich Wilhelm III, thus temporarily interrupting the rise of the young Prussian state. The King and his consort, Queen Luise, fled to distant Königsberg, the troops garrisoned in the city were removed from the abandoned capital. On 17th October 1806, the Governor, Graf Friedrich Wilhelm von der Schulenburg, had a notice posted containing two sentences which were to become famous: "The King has lost a battle. Preserving peace and quiet must now be every citizen's foremost duty."

A few days later, on 27th October, at four o'clock in the afternoon, the Emperor Napoleon rode through the Brandenburg Gate (19). The event was reported the following day in the newspaper "Vossische Zeitung": "The booming of cannons and the peal of church bells announce his arrival. An immense crowd greeted His Imperial and Royal Majesty with the liveliest attestations of joy. His Excellency General Hülin, Commandant of this capital, presented to His Majesty the Emperor members of the magistrate and the nobility, along with the most prominent citizens of the town who had gathered for this purpose at the Brandenburg Gate..." It must be remembered though when reading this euphoric report that the "Vossische Zeitung" had been placed under French trusteeship. According to other sources, a French officer rode up to the grandstand which had been erected on the side of the Gate facing towards the city, and called to the assembled dignitaries that His Majesty had decreed that, upon his passage, the gentlemen were to remove their hats. Whereupon a court counsellor by the name of Schmidt loudly shouted across the square: "He can whistle for it!"

Berliners groaned under the burden of the occupation which now followed. French soldiers, officers and civil servants were billeted in their houses. On 1st November 1806, 60.000 Frenchmen were quartered in private homes, public buildings and other housing facilities, while the Berlin population did not number more than 170.000. With the beginning of 1807, citizens who did not provide accomodations had to pay a 'quartering fee'. Only in December 1808 did the occupying troops leave Berlin.

As an added humiliation to the city, Napoleon ordered the Quadriga to be taken down from the Brandenburg Gate and shipped to Paris as a trophy (20–22). A delegation headed by Schadow tried to prevent the removal, and on 17th November 1806 submitted a petition to the Emperor, but without succes. That day, Schadow writes in a letter: "About an hour ago, M. Denon came to see me and informed me that the Emperor had given order to take down the Quadriga from the Brandenburg Gate and to convey it to France; I had to give him Jury's address; he is going to Potsdam tomorrow and will probably bring him back so that he may take down the entire group..."

Thus, early in December of 1806, coppersmith Emanuel Jury set about his sad task, took down the Quadriga from the Gate and packed it into twelve cases which on 21st December were shipped by water via Hamburg to Paris. In mid May of 1807, the booty arrived in the city on the Seine, along with other captured works of art. The "Frankfurter Journal" of 22nd May 1807 reports: "Unloading began in St. Nicholas-Port of 80 to 100 colossal cases containing antiques from Berlin and Potsdam along with the Quadriga which used to be seen on top of the Brandenburg Gate at Berlin."

Originally, Napoleon had planned to place the Quadriga on a triumphal arch which was to be specially erected; later, however, he decreed that it should adorn the St. Denis-Gate at Paris. Neither of these plans was realised though. But at least the French repaired the damages the Quadriga had suffered during transport.

Meanwhile in Berlin, the iron staff which had served as support to the Victoria, pointed accusingly skywards. According to an anecdote, Friedrich Ludwig Jahn, founder of physical education, asked one of his students what he felt at the sight of the denuded Gate. When told that the student felt nothing, Jahn is said to have boxed his ears and instructed him as follows: "From now on you will remember that we must do everything to get the Quadriga back."

This, however, was still to take years. But resistance against the occupation grew among the people. In his famous 'Addresses to the German Nation', philosopher Johann Gottlieb Fichte called for a spiritual revival of the people, a free and united country as well as deliverance from foreign rule. The Brandenburg Gate and the abducted Quadriga became national symbols for this struggle for freedom. But only after Napoleon's Grande Armée had suffered a devastating defeat in Russia was the time ripe for a national effort towards liberation. In 1813 Prussia, Austria and Russia joined forces. The subsequent Wars of Liberation, waged jointly by the Three Powers, culminated in the famous Battle of the Nations near Leipzig on 24th October 1813, in which Napoleon was decisively beaten.

In early 1814, the Berlin gazette "Neue Fakkeln" (New Torches) printed the following verses:

O Friedrich Wilhelm, do not leave
This chariot to the enemy!
That's what we ask thee, even if we
Had to carry it all the way from Paree.
And remounted on the Gate, o chariot,
We will rejoice and give thanks on the spot...

This wish was gratified by Prussian General Blücher, whom Berliners had named 'Marshal Onward'. He brought about the immediate return of the Quadriga. Her homecoming turned into a triumphal procession (23–26). Packed in fifteen cases which were loaded on six heavy carts, the Quadriga was drawn by fifty-two horses via Brussels and Aix-la-Chapelle to Düsseldorf, where six ferries carried her across the Rhine. From there, the "Berlinische Nachrichten" (Berlin News) reported on 19th May 1814: "Several hours before the arrival, the area surrounding the new port was crowded with people. As soon as the carts on which this work of art is being transported, came into view on the opposite bank of the river, they were welcomed from this side with cries of joy and ... were received by the town dignitaries assembled on the river bank, while cannons boomed and all bells were ringing ... In the Karlsstadt suburb, the procession was received with military fanfares by the garrison troops lined up in parade and presenting arms. After each musical piece, the people cheered first their beloved King Friedrich Wilhelm, then the Allied Monarchs, joined in defending the cause of humanity and, finally, everyone having German blood running in German veins..."

Covered with wreaths, garlands, poems and patriotic inscriptions, the Quadriga arrived at Zehlendorf near Berlin on 8th June, where it was unpacked and reassembled. An enthusiastic crowd numbering several thousands of people lined the way when on 30th June, the four-horse-chariot was brought to Berlin to be raised once again to its accustomed place. For a time, however, the chariot group was covered by tent-like roofing required to execute the King's wish that the emblem on the staff of the Goddess of Victory be changed. Following a design by Karl Friedrich Schinkel, the Iron Cross, a prestigious Prussian order, set within a wreath of oak leaves was manufactured in the workshop of coppersmith Jury and mounted on top of the staff, while a Prussian eagle spread its wings over it (27). With that, Eirene, Goddess of Peace, had definitely changed into Victoria, Goddess of Victory. The appropriate moment to unveil the returned Quadriga came when King Friedrich Wilhelm III, heading his victorious army, arrived at the Brandenburg Gate on 7th August 1814 (28).

Berlin "Biedermeier"

In 1815, the Congress of Vienna redefined borders all over the map of Europe. Peace returned, and after all those years of war and upheaval, all matters private and seemingly non-political took precedence. It was the era of the so-called Biedermeier, the years between Romanticism and Realism, between religious fervour and national disillusionment. In those years, for the people of Berlin an excursion to Tiergarten Park was an established part of social life (29—35). The poet E.T.A. Hoffmann, in his "Ritter Gluck" (Knight Gluck), describes the colourful scene: "Late autumn in Berlin usually still offers a number of fine days. A friendly sun steps out from the clouds and soon takes away the damp from the soft air wafting through the streets. Then a colourful procession can be observed — dandies, burghers with their spouses and little ones, all in their Sunday finery; clergymen, jewesses, young barristers, prostitutes, professors, milliners, ballerinas, officers and so forth, moving along 'Unter den Linden' towards Tiergarten." And poet Moritz Saphir wrote in his "A Drive to Charlottenburg": "... and so I drove ... straight through the Gate upon which the Victoria, as beautiful as victory itself and shining like the remembrance of all the victories in which Prussia carried off the prize, stood in glorious splendour. There is no more awe-inspiring sight than the Goddess with her head gilded by the setting sun so that she stands transfigured and with a halo, while the rosy evening light is flooding through the majestic pillars of the towering Gate..."

At that time, the quadrangle between the Brandenburg Gate and the boulevard "Unter den Linden" which, till then, had simply been called "The Quarré" because of its form, received its current name: Pariser Platz (Paris Square) in memory of the victory over Napoleon.

In 1816, the Brandenburg Gate had to be renovated once again. At a cost of 1.318 thalers, various repairs were executed. One particular problem was dealt with by the Ministerial Building Commission in a letter of 15th March 1824, to Police Headquarters, which was requested "to take appropriate action against any defilement of this eminently beautiful structure". Underlying the request was the increased posting of bills on the pillars of the Gate. That didn't look good, of course, particularly at special occasions, as for instance on 28th November 1823, when future King Friedrich Wilhelm IV welcomed his bride, the Princess Elisabeth von Bayern, at the Brandenburg Gate. And so, on 1st April 1824, Police Headquarters issued instructions to the effect that the commandant enjoin the guards to impede any posting of bills. At the same time, a notice was published in all newspapers of the city warning that perpetrators would be fined one thaler or be subject to "equivalent bodily punishment".

On 11th June 1840, funeral services were held in Berlin Cathedral for King Friedrich Wilhelm III, who had died on 7th June. The subsequent nocturnal procession taking the coffin to the mausoleum in the park of Charlottenburg Palace was described by a witness as follows: "The procession started at 11 p.m.... The air was completely still, the gaslights in the streets had not been lit, a partially clouded moon spread an elegiac light; a touching silence was observed by the enormous mass of people in attendance. A human barrier formed by the Garde du Corps and by Uhlans kept the way clear. The procession moved along the centre lane of "Unter den Linden" which is normally closed to all vehicles. On this unpaved lane, horses and hearse advanced without a sound, while torches cast an unreal glow on the intertwined treetops overhead. Thus the funeral procession passed through the centre arch of the Brandenburg Gate and continued slowly and solemnly on its darkly shaded route, lined all the way by silent crowds of people."

An epoch had come to an end, but expectations were great when Friedrich Wilhelm IV took over the government. At first, the young king appeared to justify them: He amnestied political prisoners, eased censorship, and granted asylum to the brothers Jacob and Wilhelm Grimm, appointing the two German scholars to the Berlin Academy of Sciences after they had been chased from Göttingen. But he was not willing to keep a promise made in 1815 to give the country a constitution. Thus it did not take long for discontent to set in, which in March 1848 culminated in revolution. Triggered by the February Revolution in France which had led to proclamation of a republic there, rioting erupted in the German States. Berliners assembled for political demonstrations outside the town's gates, primarily in "Den Zelten" (The Tents) in the Tiergarten Park. On 14th March 1848, about ten thousand demonstrators marched from there through the Brandenburg Gate to the Royal Palace in order to present an "Address to the King" containing their demands for political reform.

But they did not get that far. Cavalry with drawn sabres scattered the demonstrators into all directions. Quickly, the situation deteriorated and barricades went up all over the city. Then, on 18th March, shots rang out. The outcome: nineteen soldiers killed and 183 dead among the rebellious citizens. Only then the King relented. On 21st March, he rode through the city wearing a black, red and golden armband, the colours of the revolutionists. He agreed that an assembly be formed which would work out a constitution for Prussia, and promised to adopt the goals of the German revolution: Freedom and unity.

The seemingly idyllic era of the "Biedermeier" had come to an abrupt end.

Three Wars

In 1861, Wilhelm I followed his deceased brother on the Prussian throne. After liberal-minded Berlin had at first placed high hopes in him, these were soon shattered when a former opponent of the revolution, Otto von Bismarck, was named Prime Minister. But then an external conflict united the adverse political forces and bridged internal differences: A dispute over the future of Schleswig-Holstein led to war with Denmark in 1864, which Germany decided in its favour in the battle of the "Düppeler Schanzen".

Famous poet Theodor Fontane was an eyewitness to the triumphal victory procession on 7th December 1864 on the Pariser Platz (36):

"Who is coming? Who, o say —
Five regiments from Düppel way.
Five regiments of the Third Corps who late
Are marching through the Brandenburg Gate:
Prince Friedrich Karl, Wrangel, Manstein,
General Roeder, General Canstein,
Five regiments from Sundewitt
Are approaching bit by bit"

The poem entitled "Einzug" (Entrance) ends with the parade reaching the statue of King Friedrich II standing "Unter den Linden":

"All is quiet, from the horses no din,
Ten thousand are looking up at him;
He slightly bows and lifts his hat:
'I concede that wasn't bad!'"

The victorious outcome of the German-Danish war strengthened the forces striving for German unity under Prussian leadership. Prussia's influence steadily increased. At the same time, since the middle of the nineteenth century the Prussian capital began to grow rapidly and to burst its old boundaries following the progressive industrialisation with its accompanying population growth.

As per 1st January 1861, a number of communities to the south, west and northwest of Berlin were incorporated. The area covered by the city increased, the town wall and its old gates became obsolete. Besides, they impeded the ever increasing traffic as well as building activities in the prospering town. The German-Danish war, however, had delayed their demolition. But finally, in 1865, town wall and gates became victims of the pick axe. Only the Brandenburg Gate remained, but plans were made to undertake structural alterations.

On 9th November 1865, Secretary of Commerce, Trade and Public Works, Graf Heinrich August Friedrich von Itzenplitz, issued the following decree: "The Royal Building Commission is requested to establish a plan, accompanied by illustrating drawings, for the structural integration of the Brandenburg Gate now that the town wall has been demolished, in order for the Gate to present a suitable and dignified appearance also when seen from Tiergarten Park. It should be borne in mind, however, that the wings which constitute an integral part of the front building are to remain, whereas the structures in between, in which stables are housed, should perhaps be torn down..."

On 26th December of the same year, Building Inspector Hermann Blankenstein submitted six plans plus one report to the Building Commission, containing propositions for the restructuring of the Gate's lateral annexes. In respect of the entire complex the introduction says: "Since it is the most important one — not only because of its architecture but also because it represents the entrance to Berlin's most splendid boulevard — it would only seem appropriate to remodel and embellish it in a way befitting the main gate of a capital city..." Blankenstein expressed himself in favour of creating openings between the Gate and its adjacent wings, and then continued: "The undersigned has let himself be guided by the concern for accommodating not only the needs of traffic while giving the entire complex a homogenous appearance, but also to give expression to the idea inherent in the Gate as a monument so that it will not appear as an idle ornament, but stand as a memorial to patriotism and to the history of our country. In the hearts of the people, the Brandenburg Gate is firmly entrenched as a monument to the Wars of Liberation because of the memories it evokes of the reconquest of the Victoria, regardless of intentions at the time of its original construction..."

There is no need going into the Blankenstein projects in detail as they were all rejected by the Ministry. It ordered the Building Commission to establish a new plan with the condition that the "two symbolic figures" — meaning the statues of Minerva and Mars — "standing in places where openings are to be cut, should receive appropriate new locations". A plan submitted by Oberhofbaurat (The Court's Chief Building Counsellor) Johann Heinrich Strack finally met with Graf von Itzenplitz's as well as the King's approval. The required 5.900 thalers for the project had already been granted, when remodelling plans had to be postponed once again. War had broken out between Prussia and Austria over the question of predominance in the "Deutsche Bund" (German Federation) which, in 1815, had replaced the old Empire shattered by Napoleon, a war which Hapsburg lost. Following tradition, the victorious Prussian army was to return to the capital through the Brandenburg Gate. But there was a problem: The iron doors of the gateways had already been removed in 1840, and since that time the Gate could not be locked. On 14th September 1866, Police Headquarters sent the following letter to the Building Commission: "In order to safeguard a smooth entrance of the troops on 20th and 21st September, and in particular to avoid possible irruption of the parade before His Majesty the King, it will be necessary to close off the Brandenburg Gate immediately after the troops have passed through, and to block the passage between the Gate and the Customs Building by means of a strong fence. As according to report the doors of the Gate no longer exist, the Building Commission is requested to temporarily equip all five archways of the Gate with sufficiently strong and at least 8 feet high lockable doors..."

Feverishly, Gate and city were decorated. In his book "Der deutsche Krieg von 1866" (The German War of 1866), Theodor Fontane describes the happy mood prevailing in those memorable days: "In the early morning of the 20th... the city stood festively adorned and ready for the welcome. The terrain chosen for the entry of the troops was, of course, the broad avenue with its many squares running between the Brandenburg Gate and the Palace... At 9 o'clock in the morning, that avenue was already filled with crowds of people in their Sunday finery moving to and fro. Pariser Platz in particular, with the rising tiers of the grandstands tightly packed, offered a splendid and lively picture. All windows of the public and private buildings were thronged with spectators, and even the roofs were filled up to the ridges. The trees along the boulevard "Unter den Linden" were occupied by the curious. At 11 o'clock the King appeared... before the Palace. Followed by the Princes and his entourage, he rode along the 'Linden' on 'Sadowa', graciously acknowledging the acclamations arising from all sides. When he reached Pariser Platz, the cheering swelled to a storm of enthusiasm... Accompanied by general rejoicing, the King passed through the Brandenburg Gate and galloped to the head of his troops... whereupon Field Marshal Graf Wrangel, leading the assembled generals, opened the defilé" (37).

When those festive days were over and the crowds had dispersed, reconstruction of the Gate finally began. The importance this project was accorded is made evident by the fact that the King himself got involved in matters of detail. Thus on 28th January 1867, he issued the following order: "As proposed in the report of 4th December last, ... I agree that the low stable and coachhouse buildings attached to the Brandenburg Gate at Berlin be demolished, and the wing buildings of said Gate be lengthened according to the drawing C enclosed herewith; that they be provided on their back sides with a row of columns and connected by architraves and a glass roof with the customs and guard building behind. Wilhelm."

Consequently, the buildings connecting the Brandenburg Gate with its two wings were removed and replaced by porticos offering a view on Tiergarten Park from either side of the Gate. The niches facing towards the city which had contained Mars and Minerva, disappeared. The statues were given new places inside the porticos, on the side-walls of the Gate.

By 1868, reconstruction was finished, the Gate ready for the next parade. It did not take long to arrive. The founding of the "Norddeutsche Bund" (North German Federation), in which Prussia predominated had advanced unification of the German States by a large step. France eyed this development across its eastern frontier with great unease. Tension between France and Prussia, which had arisen over Prussia's attitude in the question of the succession to the Spanish throne, finally led to France's declaring war on 9th July 1870.

Only a month and a half later, the French were vanquished. In the battle of Sedan on 2nd September 1870, they received a crushing blow. "What a fortunate turn by the guidance of God", Wilhelm I telegraphed the Queen. A quarter of a century later, when the 25th anniversary of the battle of Sedan was celebrated, this phrase was chosen to adorn the Brandenburg Gate (44). On 18th January 1871, the King of Prussia was proclaimed German "Kaiser" (Emperor) in the Hall of Mirrors at the Palace of Versailles. Bismarck had attained his goal: Germany was united. On 16th June 1871, for the third time within seven years, victorious Prussian troops paraded through Berlin (38, 39).

"Those who did not experience these great and sublime hours", an eyewitness reported, "will never understand the proud happiness, the exuberant joy which had seized the city. From the roof of a house on Pariser Platz... I watched this unparalleled spectacle. I still see before me, drenched in pure sunlight, the immense crowds, the grandstands, the masts, the sea of flags, the garlands, the triumphal arches and the people — radiant, happy, cheering people... Bismarck, crowned with laurels and flanked by [his generals] Moltke and Roon, rides through the Brandenburg Gate. And behind these three historic personages who forged the German Reich, the Emperor comes into view, then the Crown Prince with his eldest son, twelve-year-old Prince Wilhelm... [and] a shower of corn flowers, lilies of the valley and roses is raining down on them. From the Lustgarten Park, the booming of salvos is heard, bells are ringing in all steeples, and the military bands are intoning 'Let Us Now Praise The Lord'..."

German patriotism had reached its peak; the people rejoiced over Germany's latest victory. And Theodor Fontane, honoring yet another return of victorious troops with a poem, rhymes:

"There they stand again, at Fritz's monument,
They look up, the old King looks at them;
He bends down, and a little gruff
Says: 'Bon soir, Messieurs, now it's enough.'"

Forty Years of Peace

The founding of the Reich was followed by an era of economic growth, the so-called "Gründerzeit" (Founding Period). Wilhelm I, who had accepted the Imperial Crown only with great reluctance, increasingly became his own legend. The people adored him, called him Wilhelm 'The Great'. When he went for drives in Tiergarten Park, people rushed up to him and cheered (40).

On 9th March 1888, the old Kaiser died, only a few days before his 91st birthday. Funeral services took place on 16th March in the Berlin Cathedral. "Vale senex imperator" — Farewell, Old Emperor — was written in large letters across the black-draped Brandenburg Gate just below the Quadriga (41, 42). When the funeral procession passed through the Gate, no one in the huge crowd suspected that they were to gather there again soon for another funeral: Wilhelm's successor, Friedrich III, died after a reign of only 99 days, on 15th June 1888. The same day, his son, aged 29, succeeded him on the throne as Kaiser Wilhelm II. The "Wilhelmian" era had begun.

Berlin grew and grew. If, in 1878, the city had just about surpassed the one-million-mark, hardly thirty years later, in 1905, it already numbered more than two million inhabitants. This explosive population growth led to a rapid expansion of the city. Particularly in what was to be known as the Westend, elegant, upper-class residential areas were developed, with wide boulevards such as the Kurfürstendamm, which took away some of the glamour of "Unter den Linden". The 'tony set' lived in Berlin W (for West). But now as before, State visitors were received at Berlin C (for Centre), meaning the Brandenburg Gate. In 1889 and again in 1892, King Umberto of Italy was welcomed there, in 1900 the old Emperor Franz Joseph of Austria, 1902 once more an Italian King, Victor Emanuel this time, followed by the Swedish, the English and the Danish Royal Couples.

Nor was the old custom of welcoming royal brides forgotten. On 3rd June 1905, Crown Princess Cäcilie was received at the Gate, and on 26th February 1906, Prince Eitel Friedrich escorted his bride, the Duchess Charlotte, from the Gate into the city. Perhaps as a reaction to this merry-go-round of occasions for pomp and circumstance, the Berlin people called the Quadriga a "four-in-hand hackney coach" (47).

The square in front of the Gate, Pariser Platz, had always been what was called a good address (46). Here, at one time or another, lived the French ambassador, composer Giacomo Meyerbeer, Prince Blücher, the painter Edward Francis Cunningham, City Counsellor and Court-appointed Master Carpenter Sommer, as well as merchant Louis Liebermann, whose son, painter Max Liebermann, later lived in the family home until his death in 1935. The house, Pariser Platz No. 7, stood to the right of the Gate when viewed from "Unter den Linden".

After his father had died in 1894, Max Liebermann returned to Berlin from a lengthy sojourn abroad and took possession of his parents' house. He asked architect Hans Grisebach to develop plans for the construction of an atelier on the roof of the building. On 29th May 1894, a request for a construction permit, supported by architect's drawings, was filed with the Surveyor's Office. Three weeks later, the Building Commission wrote a letter to the Prefect of Police pointing out "that it may safely be said that the projected atelier would be detrimental to the Brandenburg Gate whose overall aspect as a monument would suffer severely". Permission for the atelier building on the roof was withheld.

On 7th March 1896, Grisebach submitted a new application for construction, since Liebermann, "in order to exercise his profession, now had to rent an atelier". A second refusal was retracted a few weeks later because it was feared that, in case it came to a law suit, the interdiction would not be upheld. But there was still no end to the dispute, as no agreement on the height of the atelier could be reached and, finally, the Minister for Public Works, Karl von Thielen, referred the matter to the Court. On 11th February 1897, the Secretary of Civilian Affairs replied as follows: "His Majesty, the Emperor and King, finds himself unable to agree with the explanations contained in Your Excellency's report of 23rd of last month, concerning permission of the Surveyor's Office for construction of a painter's atelier on the 3rd floor of the house on Pariser Platz No. 7..." On a drawing accompanying the letter, the Emperor himself had crossed out the atelier structure and marked it with the epithet "awful". Unaware of his Sovereign's opinion, Liebermann filed suit against the interdiction and eventually won after appealing a first, unfavourable decision. On 22nd April 1898, a building permit was finally granted and Liebermann was able to erect his atelier.

For a while, it looked as if construction of an atelier on top of the Liebermann house would not remain the only building project for Pariser Platz, as it was felt at the beginning of the new century that more outlets would have to be created for the lively traffic of a large city. Plans were developed to either remodel the buildings to the right and left of the Brandenburg Gate by giving them archways, or to tear them down altogether. In a 1908 edition of the "Berliner Illustrirte Zeitung" it said: "Pariser Platz and Brandenburg Gate in Berlin are to be remodelled. This idea has sprung up all of a sudden and is now already discussed as if there really was an urgent need for such a measure, although there is no evidence of excessive traffic on Pariser Platz. But if a remodelling is to take place, preference should be given to any plan which would require the least change in the appearance of the Brandenburg Gate..." The Academy of Architecture opened a competition for the project, and in view of the proposals submitted, it was lucky that none of them were ever carried out (49—53). Both the Brandenburg Gate and Pariser Platz were able to cope with traffic without any remodelling.

Twice more, the Langhans masterpiece served as a grandiose backdrop for a display of imperial splendour: In May 1913, at the wedding of the Emperor's daughter, Princess Viktoria Luise, and Prince Ernst August, Duke of Braunschweig and Lüneburg, and in June of the same year during jubilee celebrations on the occasion of the 25th anniversary of Kaiser Wilhelm II's reign (58, 59). These festivities brought European nobility into the city in full force. Among the guests were Tsar Nikolaus II of Russia and King George V of England. Peace still prevailed. But only one year later, the shots rang out at Sarajevo which were to trigger a world conflict.

False Start of a Republic

With Germany declaring war on Russia on 1st August 1914, the First World War began (60). What was supposed to be a short victorious campaign turned into a four-year struggle of nations which cost the lives of millions of people and, in Germany, brought an end to the monarchy. When the war started, there was great enthusiasm and a willingness to sacrifice among the people. But as victories became more rare and food supplies in the Reich grew scarce, resistance against continuation of the war increased. Socialists and communists demanding a quick cessation of the fighting met with growing sympathy. Mutinies occurred and, finally, revolution broke out. On 9th November 1918, Chancellor Prince Max von Baden announced: "The Emperor and King has decided to renounce the throne." The war was lost. Wilhelm II fled to Holland. Social democrat Friedrich Ebert took over as Chancellor of the Reich.

Berlin seethed with unrest. Insurgents waving red flags marched through the city. Twice on that 9th of November a new state was called out: While social democrat Philipp Scheidemann proclaimed the German Republic from the balcony of the Reichstag (Parliament Building), communist Karl Liebknecht cheered a Free Socialist Republic of Germany from the balcony of the Royal Palace. In the ensuing weeks and months, nearly day by day formations of radicalised left-wing and right-wing forces passed through the Brandenburg Gate: Returning war veterans and Spartakists, demonstrators of all colours and monarchist volunteer corps (63–66). Time and again, civil-war-like excesses and bloody shootings occurred at which occasionally the mighty edifice itself was involved in the melée (67, 68). Then again, on 3rd March 1919, the people of Berlin assembled peacefully on Pariser Platz, which only recently had heatedly been fought over, to cheer troops returning from German East Africa, led by General Paul von Lettow-Vorbeck and Governor Heinrich Schnee (69).

Culmination of the chaos prevailing in those days came in March 1920, when the Spartakists tried once more to take over the State. In its defence, the Marine Brigade Ehrhardt, lead by its regimental band and flying the Imperial war banner, marched through the Brandenburg Gate (73) on 3rd March, thus triggering the putsch by rightist Wolfgang Kapp, which, however, collapsed after a few days. When the troops involved in the putsch retreated on 18th March, a bloody incident occurred — once again at the Brandenburg Gate — when nervous soldiers fired into the crowd of onlookers. Twelve dead and thirty injured were the sad result (74).

After the Spartakist revolt finally had been put down, Berliners were at last able to return to everyday life, even if that meant the often hectic and chaotic way of life of the twenties: Economic prosperity and a great variety of cultural activities on the one hand; inflation, mass unemployment, scandals, assassination attempts and extreme radicalisation and polarisation on the other.

Occasions at which the Brandenburg Gate would serve as a festive backdrop were rare during the years of the Weimar Republic. No Kaiser to ride through the centre passage, no princesses to welcome; only now and then a military parade. But on 11th May 1925, the new President of the Reich, Paul von Hindenburg, made his entrance into the city through the Gate, and the heads of state who visited Berlin in those years — e.g. the Shah of Afghanistan in 1928 and King Fuad of Egypt in 1929 — also entered the capital of the Reich through the Brandenburg Gate (78).

Before that, in the summer of 1926, the Gate underwent a general renovation. To this end, it had been sheathed in a compact wooden scaffolding which also solidly encased the Quadriga (75), thus prompting the people to speak of "Berlin's most elevated stables". Horses though had become scarce in Berlin. They had been pushed aside by the automobile, taxis had taken over from hackney coaches. This drastic change in his trade caused coachman Gustav Hartmann to set out on a spectacular drive, in 1928, from Berlin to Paris and back. The Berlin press heavily emphasised the friendship-between-the-nations aspect of his journey. After all, the wounds of the First World War had not yet healed, and the Foreign Secretaries of former arch enemies France and Germany, Aristide Briand and Gustav Stresemann, had considerable difficulties to arrive at less strained relations between their peoples. When coachman Gustav Hartmann (surnamed "Iron Gustav") returned to Berlin through the Brandenburg Gate, Pariser Platz was jammed with one oft the biggest crowds of spectators it had ever seen (77).

In October 1929, Gustav Stresemann, the most distinguished statesman of the Weimar Republic, died. Hundreds of thousands of people lined the streets when the funeral procession passed through the Brandenburg Gate (79). And one or the other of the onlookers may even have felt with a pang that he was not only witnessing the funeral of a great statesman but also that of the Republic.

But the Gate did not only serve as a backdrop for occasions of state, it was also a favourite subject for the fine arts which flourished during the Weimar Republic. Quite a number of artists painted the Brandenburg Gate: Lesser Ury (62), Ernst Ludwig Kirchner (80), Conrad Felixmüller, Oskar Kokoschka (81), Hans Baluschek (82), or Felix Nussbaum (83), to name just a few. In his painting "Der tolle Platz" (The Mad Square) showing a destroyed Liebermann house and a broken victory column, Nussbaum, who died in Auschwitz in 1944, was not expressing any premonitions but rather attacking the conservative spirit reigning at the Academy of Fine Arts. Theo Matejko's charcoal drawing of 1933, on the other hand, depicts — in scary clairvoyance — what twelve years later was to become reality: Death and destruction would come over Berlin, and the Brandenburg Gate would fall into ruin (89).

"By the Light of Flaming Torches"

The world depression, mass unemployment and the inability of the democratic parties to get the situation under control, as well as increasing radicalisation on the left and on the right dealt the Weimar Republic the death blow. On 30th January 1933, Hitler held his entrance in the Reichskanzlei (Chancellery). To celebrate the "Machtergreifung" (Seizing of power), Joseph Goebbels, future Minister of Propaganda, had organised a three-and-a-half-hour torch parade, consisting of national-socialist and German-nationalist formations marching through the Brandenburg Gate and along the Wilhelmstraße. "It is almost like a dream...", Goebbels later described his impressions. "We are standing upstairs, at the window, while by the light of flaming torches hundreds of thousands of people are marching past the aged President of the Reich and the young Chancellor, calling out their gratitude and their joy..." When the photographs of the torch parade came out too dark to be used for propaganda purposes, Goebbels had stills made from the movie "Hans Westmar", the life-story of 'martyred' Nazi Horst Wessel, for which the event was reenacted in the summer of 1933 (87, 88).

But in the night of 28th February 1933, it was the burning Reichstag-building rather than the light of torches which cast an eerie glow on the Brandenburg Gate (90). Though the arsonist, 24-year-old Dutch communist Marinus van der Lubbe, had acted on his own, the Nazis gladly took advantage of the deed and ordered the first big wave of arrests among their political adversaries. Nation-wide, five thousand opponents were rounded up to disappear in camps and prisons. And when the Emergency Decree "For the Protection of People and State" was issued shortly thereafter, the most important basic rights outlined in the Weimar constitution became null and void.

One week later, elections to the Reichstag (parliament) were held, after which — despite massive attempts at intimidation — the Hitler party had not obtained the absolute majority. But together with its German-nationalist coalition partner, it did reach 51.9 per cent. The opening session of the newly elected Reichstag on 21st March 1933 was celebrated in Potsdam with enormous pomp. On the evening of that day, once more tens of thousands of Nazis marched in a torch parade through the Brandenburg Gate (91) which henceforth was to witness an increasing succession of défilés of Nazi-formations of all kinds (94, 95).

Through political terror on the one hand, and shrewdly organised mass spectacles and successful measures against unemployment on the other, the Nazis were soon able to create an appearance of calm and prosperity. The Olympic Games of 1936, hosted by Berlin, served as a welcome opportunity for showing off. The capital of the Reich was swept and garnished, and from 1st to 16th August, a grandiose spectacle was offered to the admiring world. The country presented itself as open-minded, peaceable and very hospitable. This had an enormous effect, internally as well as externally, which was reinforced by the first systematic use of radio broadcasting.

Once more, the Brandenburg Gate found itself in the midst of the hub. Not only was it featured on the official poster for the Games (98), but — generously hung with Olympic flags and garlands (99–101) — it pointed the way from the city to the splendidly situated Olympic grounds to the masses of visitors.

In connection with the preparations for the Olympic Games, a grave accident occurred near the Brandenburg Gate. At Ebertstraße, then Hermann-Göring-Straße, a construction site for an underground section of the S-Bahn collapsed because of insufficient safety precautions, costing the lives of nineteen people (97).

One year after the Olympic Games, in August 1937, celebration of Berlin's 700-year anniversary gave occasion for a magnificent procession through the city and, of course, through the Brandenburg Gate, once again decorated with garlands. The entire city had turned out to watch (102, 103), little realising that it was already doomed.

In September 1937, Italian Duce Benito Mussolini made his entrance into Berlin through the Brandenburg Gate. The bombastic reception — elaborate decorations and a sea of flags had turned "Unter den Linden" into a triumphal route of German national socialism and Italian fascism (105) — was a foreboding of the dictators' rising megalomania. Where their way would lead, became blatantly evident in 1938, when the Legion Condor which had fought in the Spanish Civil War, marched through what used to be the Gate of Peace (107), and when on 1st October the so-called liberation of the Sudetenland was celebrated with an imposing 'Dome of Light', which illuminated the night sky over the Gate (108).

On 20th April 1939, Hitler celebrated his 50th birthday with a formidable military parade along the broad avenue leading west from the Brandenburg Gate (109). In their minds, he and his followers had long since crossed national borders to conquer "Lebensraum" (space to live) in the east and build a world empire, for which, however, present day Berlin would be too small to serve as a capital. So the old capital of Prussia and of the German Reich was to be made into the world capital "Germania". Hitler's "Generalbauinspektor für die Reichshauptstadt" (General Building Inspector for the Capital of the Reich), Albert Speer, designed gigantic buildings by far surpassing human scale (110, 111).
A "Hall of the People" which was to be erected next to the Reichstag, would have doomed the parliament building and the Brandenburg Gate to total insignificance. But on 1st September 1939, Hitler brought on the Second World War, and his plans for a world capital never got off the paper.

Followed the campaigns against Poland and France: On 18th July 1940, victorious troops once again marched through the Brandenburg Gate and were cheered by the Berlin population — not so much out of enthusiasm for the war but from a feeling of relief over the quick victories (114, 115). But then, in 1943, the bombing of Berlin started, and there was no more cause for cheering (118). Borough after borough fell to ruin, thousands lost their lives.

With the attack on the Soviet Union and the thrust of the German troops towards the Caucasus, Hitler was finally overreaching himself. The German defeat in the battle of Stalingrad was followed by the steady advance of the Red Army. Meanwhile the last resources of the country were mobilised. Even the copper sheeting of the roof of the as yet intact Brandenburg Gate was taken down in February of 1943 as it had become "material necessary to the war effort".

When in February 1945 the Red Army crossed the Oder River, bombed-out Berlin still had a population of 2.8 million people. On 16th April 1945, the signal for the last offensive was given. The battle of Berlin had begun: 22.000 guns and hundreds of fighter planes fired away at the last defensive positions of the German Wehrmacht, surrounding the capital of the Reich. At about noon of the 21st April, the first shells hit Pariser Platz and the boulevard "Unter den Linden". On 30th April, Soviet soldiers stormed the Reichstag and hoisted the Soviet flag on the cupola of the burnt-out parliament building. On the same day, Hitler committed suicide in the bunker of the nearby Reichskanzlei (Chancellery). On 1st May, the Brandenburg Gate, which had been heavily barricaded and turned into an anti-tank blockade (119), was stormed by Soviet troops. Soon the red Flag (121–123) was also flying over the severely battered Quadriga.

Cold War

The battle of Berlin was over, the German Wehrmacht had capitulated. With the completely ruined city and the heavily damaged Brandenburg Gate as a ghostly backdrop, units of the Red Army held their victory parade (124, 125). The former capital with its four million inhabitants had sunk into a chaos of 75 million cubic metres of rubble, equalling one seventh of the total debris of the German Reich. Traffic of any kind had broken down, as had the supply of water, gas and electricity. It was to take months and years before life in Berlin returned to normal.

In Tiergarten Park, close to the Brandenburg Gate, the Soviets erected a memorial to their fallen soldiers. It was consecrated on 11th November 1945, the anniversary of the October-Revolution. At that time, the Soviets were no longer the only victorious power occupying Berlin. On 4th July, British and American troops had moved into the sectors which had been allocated to them (127), French units followed in August.

Every day life in Berlin was marked by want and destitution. Catastrophic shortages led to the rise of black markets on which lively commerce developed between the Berlin population and the occupying forces. One of the best-known markets was held in the area surrounding the Brandenburg Gate (130). In view of the critical supply situation, Mayor Arthur Werner, whom the Soviets had installed, on 15th February 1946 appealed to the Berlin population to use every available square metre of ground for the cultivation of vegetables. As a consequence, Tiergarten Park was almost completely cleared of trees and divided into small gardening plots (134). These efforts at farming around the Brandenburg Gate met with considerable success: At a Thanksgiving ceremony in the fall of 1946 it was announced that 20.000 cwt. of vegetables and potatoes had been harvested. Prizes were awarded for a fifty-pound pumpkin, a three-pound savoy cabbage and a tomato plant bearing 76 fruits.

But this idyll in the heart of Berlin was deceptive. Within the city, the so-called "Cold War" was gathering momentum. The differing interests of the former Allies clashed and led to confrontations between the three Western Allies on the one hand and the Soviet Union on the other. When the three Western Powers decided to unite the economies of their zones, and on 20th June 1948 implemented a monetary reform, Stalin immediately took his revenge on the three Western Sectors of Berlin by initiating a total blockade. For eleven months, half of the city was supplied by air; only then did the Soviets give in.

But the rift that went through Germany and its capital deepened. On 24th May 1949, the "Grundgesetz" (the constitution on which the Federal Republic of Germany is based), went into effect, while on 7th October of the same year the German Democratic Republic was founded. The Western Sectors of Berlin became a Bundesland (State of the Federation), whereas the Eastern Sector became the capital of the GDR. And suddenly, the Brandenburg Gate, the Gate of Peace, found itself standing on a border-line. Though traffic back and forth was still possible, the two halves of the city drifted farther and farther apart, evolving in accordance with the two States and the two political systems they now belonged to. While the West experienced its economic miracle, the East groaned under Soviet demands for reparations and the restrictions of a planned economy.

When on 16th June 1953 the East German government further increased the already elevated work norms, spontaneous work stoppages occurred which, on 17th June, escalated into a people's uprising against the communist regime. In Berlin young workers climbed the Brandenburg Gate, took down the red Flag and burned it (138—140). Then, carrying black, red and golden flags and singing the German national anthem, they marched through the Gate towards the West Sectors (141). The Soviet City Commandant declared a state of emergency for East Berlin, Russian tanks were placed strategically all over the city, and together with the GDR's People's Police, the "Glorious Red Army" quelled the revolt which left more than 260 dead. Twenty-one demonstrators were shot on the spot under martial law, about twenty party functionaries, members of the People's Army and State Security Agents were lynched by angry crowds. Roughly 20 000 people were detained for interrogation, 3 000 of whom were later sentenced to prison.

"There is no power on earth which could permanently lower the German people into a people of slaves", West Berlin Governing Mayor Ernst Reuter declared, and then continued: "We shall show the world that it is possible to deal even with a totalitarian regime, by our determination to reach our goal no matter what the circumstances: The goal of our national unity, the goal of our freedom and the goal sacred to us all and dear to our hearts: Peace for the world..." And the "New York Times" wrote on 18th June: "... we now know, and the world knows, that within the German people a courage and a spirit are alive which will not tolerate suppression forever."

The icier the Cold War between East and West became, the deeper also the cut caused by the division of Germany and Berlin. In East Germany, common German history was systematically negated or swept under the carpet, and any vestiges which might keep memories alive were destroyed. Thus in 1950, GDR Chief of State Walter Ulbricht ordered the Royal Palace in Berlin to be razed. To the new rulers, the old residence of the Hohenzollern appeared as a symbol of all that was hateful: Prussia and the values it stood for. Though the huge palace complex was badly damaged by bombs, it would have been possible to save this largest of all profane baroque buildings north of the Alps.

The Brandenburg Gate almost suffered a similar fate. Rumors of an imminent demolition of the Langhans structure circulated in the years 1946 and 1947. But on 17th November 1949 the newspaper "Telegraf am Abend" (Evening Telegraph) announced: "For some time now, every good Berliner has been worried by rumors concerning the Brandenburg Gate. The unfortunate plan to tear it down altogether has meanwhile been definitely abandoned. Luckily, the Gate sustained very little damage and can easily be repaired. The Gate's Quadriga, the four-horse-chariot created by Schadow, is in worse condition though. It was so badly damaged during the war that it will almost be impossible to restore it. And there is already talk that the Quadriga will be replaced by another statue."

In May 1950 the battered remains of the Quadriga were removed by brigades of the "Freie Deutsche Jugend" (Free German Youth). For the first time since the days of Napoleon, the roof of the Brandenburg Gate, severely damaged and only recently scantily secured, was bare once more. In place of the Schadow-group now stood a mast on which a red flag was flying.

Measures to secure the Gate could only be of a temporary nature. In September 1956, East Berlin decided to thoroughly renovate the Langhans structure and again to adorn it with a crowning statue. Fortunately, the idea to erect a monumental pair of "Socialist Activists" in place of the Quadriga was dropped. Instead, a rather surprising thing happened: At the height of the Cold War, then East Berlin Head Mayor Friedrich Ebert jun. wrote a letter to his West Berlin counterpart asking him to lend them the plaster casts of the chariot group. These had been taken from the original just before the bombings and were now kept in the State Museum at Berlin-Charlottenburg. At a press conference in East Berlin it was announced that reconstruction of the Gate was part of a master plan to improve the capital of the GDR. Termination of the necessary work was forecast for the end of 1957.

The West Berlin side was, of course, pleased with the reconstruction plans, but handing over the irreplaceable plaster casts was out of the question. And so Mayor Franz Amrehn informed his East Berlin colleague at the end of September 1956 that West Berlin would prefer renewing an offer Ernst Reuter had made in 1950, i.e. have the Quadriga reconstructed at the expense of the West Berlin Senate. As soon as work on the Gate was finished, the new chariot-group would be turned over to East Berlin authorities. Though East German newspaper "Neues Deutschland" called the letter an insult, both halves of the city went through with the deal.

On 14th December 1957, while a chilling wet snow was falling, the topping out ceremony took place in East Berlin. In front of the Gate which was still surrounded by scaffolding, a grandstand adorned with garlands had been erected from which East Berlin Vice-Mayor Waldemar Schmidt launched new attacks against the ideological enemy in the western half of the city (144, 145): "If the West Berlin Senate had seen fit to lend us the plaster casts last year", he shouted, "we would probably have been able to already begin mounting the Quadriga today. But those frontier-town politicians had their own ideas. The whole world is witness to the ignominious spectacle showing that not even restoration of this landmark of our city is exempt from the Cold War but is used as a means of agitation against the Workers' and Peasants' State."

And bricklayers' foreman Tietz 'topped' things off: "On this day of topping out we vow to do everything in our power to keep these buildings of a great cultural tradition from ever again falling victim to an imperialist war. We also vow to defend the banner of freedom raised in May 1945 by the glorious Soviet Army as a symbol of victory."

While on Pariser Platz one propagandistic phrase chased the other, artisans at the foundry of Hermann Noack at West Berlin suburb Friedenau grappled with some unexpected problems (146–155). For not only were they to ensure that the Quadriga would be a true replica of the original, they also had to eliminate certain technical defects due to the 18th century manufacturing process. Thus their use of heavier sheet copper required new statics and necessitated replacement of the 5-centimetre iron bars holding the Quadriga by a 7-centimetre steel support. To increase the equilibrium of the group it was necessary to give several of the horses' legs a little twist. Lastly, the entire steel construction had to be coated with three layers of a synthetic resin as protection against climatic damages. These measures increased cost from the forecast DM 150 000 to DM 250 000.

At the end of July 1958, the Quadriga was at last ready (156). When Noack's workers prepared its disassembled parts to be transported by crane and flat-bed truck to the Brandenburg Gate where they were to be put together, East Berlin authorities prohibited the mounting of the group by its West Berlin manufacturer. All he was allowed to do was to move the monumental horses together with the Goddess of Victory and her chariot from West to East through the Gate and to unload them on Pariser Platz (157, 158). Several hundred onlookers immediately gathered and cheered the old Berlin symbol of liberty and peace. Even East Berlin Mayor Friedrich Ebert jun. showed up to have himself photographed in front of the copper foursome. But before his arrival, the emblems of the victory goddess, i.e. the Iron Cross and the Eagle, those old Prussian symbols which, since the return of the Quadriga in 1814, had been integral parts of the statue, were covered with a sack (160).

This took place on Friday, 1st August 1958. On Monday, 4th August 1958, the frontpage headline of the tabloid "BZ" hit like a bomshell: "The Quadriga Stolen! Overnight Disappearance in East Berlin." Whereabouts of the goddess and her four-horse-chariot was, however, soon disclosed by a bulletin in officialese issued by the West Berlin Senate: "The still not sufficiently explained transfer of the Quadriga to the Marstall (the former Royal Stables) constitutes... a flagrant breach — not even contested by Eastern authorities — of the agreements concluded between the two Commissioners and is without a doubt illegal. Even before delivery, the request for a formal and official transfer, which would have allowed free disposal of the artwork, had been refused, whereupon negotiating a transfer was no longer made a preliminary for its employ. As a consequence, Eastern Sector Authorities are only entitled to an immediate installation of the Quadriga on top of the Gate. Therefore, any other employ or relocation constitute an infringement of rights. To this hour, an explanation as to the true motives behind the policy of the official agencies could not be obtained."

The reason for the temporary housing of the monument in the courtyard of the old Marstall (161) turned out to be the following: The socialist regime could not abide the Prussian Eagle and the Iron Cross and had these "symbols of Prussian and German militarism" removed under cover of darkness. Suggestions for possible replacements included: A peace dove in place of the eagle; a Soviet star; a five-point star; hammer and sickle, or the GDR-emblem of hammer and a pair of compasses to replace the Iron Cross (159). No agreement could be reached on any of these though and so, until the Quadriga was taken down for yet another repair in the spring of 1990, a provisional solution prevailed: Eagle and Iron Cross were removed and deposited in the East Berlin "Märkische Museum". Henceforth, the top of the staff held by the Victoria was adorned only by the empty oak wreath.

Yet Berlin rejoiced when on 28th September 1958, a beautiful autumn day, it was able to celebrate the mounting of the Quadriga which, it was hoped, would be leading the way towards more peaceful times (162, 163). And it seemed indeed as if life around the Brandenburg Gate ran its quiet and normal course. State visitors came as before and looked from one side across to the other; the Schöneberger Choir Boys sang Christmas carols under a lighted tree at the foot of the Quadriga; Soviet soldiers had their picture taken in front of the Gate, and U.S. movie director Billy Wilder even shot his film "One, Two, Three" there (164–167), starring James Cagney, Liselotte Pulver, Horst Buchholz and Hans Lothar. The film was a satire on East and West and Coca-Cola. Because of the delicate political situation, the real Brandenburg Gate could not play its intended part. Wilder did not even try to negotiate for a permission to shoot with East Berlin officials — he was not ready for any compromise whatever. And so a copy of the Gate, Pariser Platz and the boulevard "Unter den Linden" was erected in the Munich film studios at Geiselgasteig at the then horrendous cost of one million Marks, and using enormous amounts of wood, plaster, paint and concrete. On 13th August 1961, the newspaper "Berliner Morgenpost" reported of the filming: "A man like Billy Wilder even beats the rain: He had his "Unter den Linden" guttered and asphalted at great expense and so made his mass scenes almost weatherproof whereas, confronted with a political low, even a Hollywood director is powerless. But Billy Wilder seems to be an optimist: Yesterday, he and his camera crew returned to Berlin for location shots." They were not to get them...

The Wall

That Sunday, 13th August 1961, the GDR-Regime began erecting a wall across Berlin, with the intention of hermetically sealing off the eastern part of the city from the west. Only a few weeks before, Walter Ulbricht had declared: "Nobody plans to build a wall." But at that very moment, preparations were already under way and running at full speed, directed by Erich Honecker. The purpose of this drakonian measure which also revealed the powerlessness of the socialist regime as well as its brutal nature, was to prevent its own citizens from fleeing to the west, thus bleeding the GDR to death. Between 1949 and 1961, about three million people had left the territory of the GDR, and 1961 in particular witnessed a dramatic increase in the number of refugees.

In the early morning hours of that August Sunday, all along the new dividing line, streets connecting East Berlin to the western part of the city were blocked by means of concrete posts and barbed wire. Uniformed "Betriebskampfgruppen" (Factory Combat Groups) in armoured cars took up position at the Brandenburg Gate (168–172). During the following days and weeks, these provisional barriers were gradually replaced by a solid wall.

In those days, unparalleled scenes could be observed: Desperate people trying to surmount the barbed wire, others jumping out the windows of houses which over night had become part of the border and had their doors walled up. GDR Border Guards with guns at the ready standing guard over the construction workers who were forced to immure themselves. On both sides of the barbed wire members of newly divided families stood waving at each other with tearful eyes, as well as thousands of helpless spectators (179). Equally helpless were the politicians and members of the military who came to the Brandenburg Gate on that 13th August and on the days that followed. First among them was West Berlin Governing Mayor Willy Brandt who interrupted an election campaign tour through the Federal Republic and, having returned to Berlin in the early morning of that infamous Sunday, immediately went to the Brandenburg Gate (176–178).

To all the memorable days in German history on which the Brandenburg Gate was the focus, another one had to be added — one of the saddest. For the first time in its existence, the Langhans structure no longer served as a town gate but had become an inaccessible building in the no-man's-land between east and west. In the following years, the cry "Open the Gate!" became the key-word whenever people gathered to demand German unity. How irrevocably a symbol of German history the Gate had become was made clear by Richard von Weizsäcker, then Governing Mayor of West Berlin, when he said: "The German question remains open for so long as the Brandenburg Gate is shut."

During the bitter years of its division, Berlin received many tokens of friendship. People from all corners of the earth came to visit, saw the wall and were shocked by the experience. Of special importance to the city and its determination to survive was President John F. Kennedy's visit to Berlin in June 1963. His words "Ich bin ein Berliner" expressed his solidarity with the inhabitants of the divided city. When he went to the Brandenburg Gate, the GDR-Regime had sheets of cloth hung across the passageways to block the view on the boulevard "Unter den Linden" (182).

Though in the course of the following years negotiations between the West Berlin Senate and the East Berlin Magistrate led to a so-called "Passierscheinabkommen" (Visiting Agreement) which allowed West Berliners occasional family visits in the eastern part of the city — e.g. at Christmas 1963 — border fortifications were further strengthened. After having reinforced and raised the Wall in the vicinity of the Brandenburg Gate in July 1966, East Berlin authorities erected a billboard bearing the following warning: "Trying to Force the State Border or Engaging in Provocative Action at the Wall Will Only Make Matters Worse!" (184). No comment required.

The city adapted and learned to live with the wall. The chorus of those still daring to shout "Open the Gate!" diminished in number and volume. In the course of the nineteen seventies, the Four-Power-Agreement on Berlin was concluded as well as an agreement between the Federal Republic and the GDR on transit routes to and from Berlin. Visiting arrangements allowing West Berliners access to the eastern part of the city were negotiated between the West Berlin Senate and the GDR Government. While shots could still be heard from the east side of the wall — at least 73 people lost their lives while attempting to flee — its west side deteriorated more and more to a mere tourist attraction, becoming the world's largest "canvas" on which painters and all those with 'artistic' inclinations could let loose. More and more, the wall became part of everyday life, with demonstrations against this inhuman structure becoming ever more infrequent (187—190).

Thus it was a rare political event when, at Berlin's 750th anniversary celebration on 12th June 1987, Ronald Reagan, President of the United States of America, stood before 25 000 Berliners assembled in front of the Brandenburg Gate, and appealed to Mikhail Gorbachev: "Mr. General Secretary, if you are seeking peace, if you want prosperity for the Soviet Union and Eastern Europe, if you are striving for liberalisation, then come to this Gate. Mr. Gorbachev, open this Gate! Mr. Gorbachev, tear down this wall!" (192). Certainly, Ronald Reagan's words, his good intentions and his optimism were much appreciated. But was there still anyone to be found in Germany and especially in Berlin who shared this optimism? Candid people will have to admit that they never expected the wall to come down two and a half years after this historical speech.

"We Are One People"

On 9th November 1989 the time had come: The socialist regime, already weakened and discredited by new waves of fleeing East Germans, collapsed. It opened the borders, and freedom-hungry GDR-citizens poured into the west. Berlin experienced some of the happiest days in its history. Exuberant people from east and west danced on the wall in front of the Brandenburg Gate (193–195). This was the very spot where the wall had to come down now, here the new freedom was to be celebrated. The Gate had been the symbol for a divided Germany for too long; from now on it would stand for the newly gained unity. For weeks to come, TV and radio crews from all over the world set up shop on the Street of 17th June, to the west of the Gate, to be present for live coverage of the official reopening of the Brandenburg Gate. Every evening thousands of Berliners gathered, shouting the old cry: "Open the Gate!" (198, 199).

On 22nd December 1989 the long wait came to an end: Chancellor Helmut Kohl, GDR Prime Minister Hans Modrow and the Mayors of the two halves of the city, Walter Momper (west) and Erhard Krack (east) finally opened a new passage through the already crumbling wall alongside the Gate, at this, Germany's most symbolic and historic site (200, 201). In his speech on Pariser Platz Momper said: "The opening of the Brandenburg Gate moves the people here in Berlin more than all the other openings of the border in recent weeks. Our hearts are attached to this building, to this site. Now that Berliners are once again able to pass through the Gate from both sides, we know for sure that life in Berlin is getting back to normal, that life in Berlin will be more exciting than before." And he concluded with the words: "Berlin, now rejoice!"

Almost half a million people gathered at the Brandenburg Gate on the evening of 31st December 1989 for the biggest New Year's Eve party the city and the country had ever seen (202, 203). That night, Berliners gave a moving testimony that, even after twenty-eight years of separation, they had not become strangers to each other. The next morning though, when Pariser Platz and the surrounding area were cleared of rubbish, a more sober mood set in. One man had been found dead, and the collapse of a huge screen had caused serious injuries to a great number of people. The Gate itself had also considerably suffered from the jubilant crowds. Its walls and columns were covered with graffiti. Rowdies had climbed the roof of the Gate, set off fire crackers and pulled off or twisted the sheet copper of the roof covering. Most of all, however, the Quadriga had suffered under the New Year's Eve onslaught: The laurel wreath had been torn from the head of the Goddess of Peace, her left arm was almost wrenched off, the horses had been kicked by many feet and their harnesses were badly damaged.

Emergency repairs were executed as early as 18th January 1990, but it soon became apparent that the entire Gate complex needed to be completely overhauled. Thus in March, the Gate was once more encased in scaffolding, and the four-horse-chariot was taken to the Berlin "Museum für Verkehr und Technik" (Museum of Traffic and Technical Science) for repairs (205–207). East and west are setting about in newfound unanimity to restore this magnificent building to its old splendour and to new glory in time for its 200th birthday on 6th August 1991. It will be the first festive occasion on which the Gate will not serve as a backdrop but will itself be the centre of attention. And it will be once more what it always was: The focus of German history.

Das alte Brandenburger Tor, wie es der Kupferstecher Daniel Chodowiecki 1764 gesehen hat (1). Aus der Mitte des 18. Jahrhunderts stammt auch die nächtliche Ansicht des alten Tors von unbekannter Künstlerhand (2).

The old Brandenburg Gate as seen by engraver Daniel Chodowiecki in 1764 (1). The nocturnal view of the old Gate by an unknown artist also dates back to the middle of the 18th century (2).

3

4

5

Die Bauzeichnung (3) hat Carl Gotthard Langhans 1789 angefertigt. Das Gemälde eines unbekannten Künstlers (4), vermutlich die früheste Darstellung des neuen Tores, dürfte vor Aufstellung der Quadriga 1793 entstanden sein, da sich das hier dargestellte Viergespann erheblich von Schadows Standbild unterscheidet. So hält die Friedensgöttin statt der Panierstange mit Trophäen einen Palmzweig in der Hand.
Die Radierung aus der Zeit um 1800 von Louis Serrurier und Peter Haas (5) zeigt das Tor von Westen her. Deutlich erkennt man die alte Stadtmauer.

The architect's drawing was done by Carl Gotthard Langhans in 1789 (3). The painting by an unknown artist (4), probably the earliest representation of the new Gate, must have been executed before the Quadriga was mounted, as the chariot group shown differs considerably from Schadow's design. The Goddess of Peace, for instance, holds a palm branch in her hand instead of the staff with the emblems. The engraving done around 1800 by Louis Serrurier and Peter Haas (5) depicts the Gate as seen from the west. The old town wall is clearly visible.

6

7

8

9

Die Reliefs für die Wände der Tordurchfahrten hat Christian Bernhard Rode entworfen. Sie zeigen Szenen aus der klassischen Herakles-Sage. Hier eine Auswahl: Herakles will Alceste aus der Unterwelt zurückführen (6); Herakles in Ägypten (7); Herakles im Nessus-Gewand (8); Herakles in Olympia (9). Die für die Angehörigen des Hofes vorbehaltene Mitteldurchfahrt ist geschmückt mit den Reliefs »Herakles befreit Herione« (10) und »Kampf mit den Kentauren« (11).

The reliefs for the walls of the passageways were designed by Christian Bernhard Rode. They show scenes from the classical Heracles legend. Here a selection: Heracles Attempting to Lead Alceste Back from the Hades (6); Heracles in Egypt (7); Heracles Clad in the Nessos Garment (8); Heracles in Olympia (9). The centre gateway reserved for members of the Court is adorned with the reliefs "Heracles Liberates Herione" (10) and "Battle With the Centaurs" (11).

10

11

Die in der nördlichen Säulenhalle stehende Statue der Minerva, der Schirmherrin der Städte, stammt von Johann David Meltzer (12). Die Statue des Kriegsgotts Mars schuf Conrad Boy nach einem Plan von Schadow (13); sie steht in der südlichen Säulenhalle. Auf einen Entwurf von Rode und Schadow geht das Attikarelief »Zug des Friedens« von Boy und Johann Christian Unger zurück (14).

Johann David Meltzer created the statue of the Minerva, patroness of cities, standing in the northern pillared hall (12). The statue of war god Mars was created by Conrad Boy after a design by Schadow (13); it stands in the southern pillared hall. The attic relief "The Procession of Peace" by Boy and Johann Christian Unger is based on a design by Rode and Schadow (14).

12

14

13

15

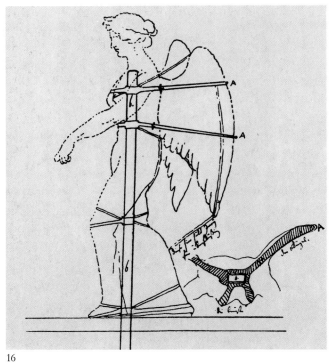
16

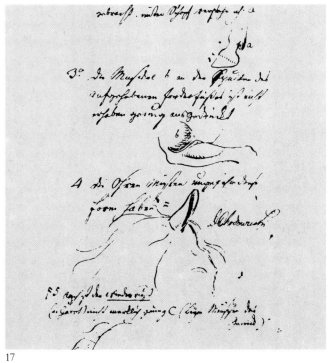
17

18

Die Darstellung von Daniel Berger aus dem Jahre 1798 (15) zeigt das den Athener Propyläen nachempfundene Tor mit der 1793 aufgestellten Quadriga. Auch das von Johann Gottfried Schadow entworfene Standbild lehnt sich an antike Vorbilder an (18). Schadows Skizzen (16, 17) stammen aus dem Jahr 1789.

This representation of 1798 (15) by Daniel Berger shows the Gate, modelled after the Athens Propylae, with the Quadriga which was mounted in 1793. The statue designed by Gottfried Schadow also takes its inspiration from classical art (18). Sketches by Schadow (16, 17) from the year 1789.

Der Einzug Kaiser Napoleons in Berlin am 27. Oktober 1806. Dieses Ölgemälde von Charles Meynier hängt im Musée de Versailles.

The entry of Emperor Napoleon into Berlin on 27th October 1806. This oil painting by Charles Meynier hangs in the Musée de Versailles.

20

21

76

Der Raub der Quadriga durch Napoleon 1806 ist eine schlimme Demütigung für Berlin und Preußen, doch wird das Schadowsche Standbild durch dieses Ereignis zu einem nationalen Symbol. Die Karikatur »Der Pferdedieb von Berlin« (20) ist um 1813, die Porzellantasse mit dem seines Schmucks beraubten Tor (21) um 1808 entstanden. Die Szene der Landsturm-Übung (22) hat Richard Knötel 1913 zur Hundertjahrfeier der Befreiungskriege lithographiert.

The abduction of the Quadriga by Napoleon in 1806 constitutes a terrible humiliation for Berlin and Prussia. But it changes the Schadow statue into a national symbol. The caricature "The Horse Thief of Berlin" (20) was done around 1813, the china cup depicting the Gate bereft of its crowning ornament (21) around 1808. The scene showing reserve troops at drill (22) was lithographed in 1913 by Richard Knötel on the occasion of centenary celebrations of the Wars of Liberation, which were fought against Napoleon's Grande Armée.

22

24

25

Die Rückkehr der Quadriga nach Berlin 1814 war ein einziger Triumphzug und fand ihren Niederschlag in zahlreichen zeitgenössischen Darstellungen: Holzstich von Rudolf Eichstaedt mit dem Titel »Victoria!« (23); Tuschzeichnung eines unbekannten Künstlers (24); Gedenktasse der Königlichen Porzellanmanufaktur Berlin (25); Kupferstich von Daniel Berger (26).

The return of the Quadriga to Berlin in 1814 turns into a triumphal procession echoed in numerous contemporary representations: Wood engraving by Rudolf Eichstaedt entitled "Victoria!" (23); china-ink drawing by an unknown artist (24); commemorative cup of the Royal China Manufacture in Berlin (25); copper engraving by Daniel Berger (26).

26

Als äußeres Zeichen ihrer neuen nationalen Würde wird die Viktoria nach ihrer Rückkehr auf Wunsch des Königs mit dem Eisernen Kreuz geschmückt (27). Die zeitgenössische Federzeichnung von Ludwig Wolf (28) zeigt den Einzug Friedrich Wilhelms III. am 7. August 1814 in Berlin. Die Quadriga steht wieder an ihrem angestammten Platz. Wie sehr die Berliner das Viergespann ins Herz geschlossen haben, zeigt die Lithographie von Theodor Hosemann aus der Zeit um 1830 (29).

As an outward sign of her new national standing, the King has the Victoria adorned with the Iron Cross upon her return (27). The contemporary pen-and-ink drawing by Ludwig Wolf (28) shows the entry of Friedrich Wilhelm III on 7th August 1814 in Berlin. The Quadriga stands in her accustomed place again. Theodor Hosemann's lithograph dating from around 1830 (29) shows how dear the four-horse-chariot had become to the Berlin population.

29

Die Bildunterschrift unter dem Original lautet: »Liebeken, können se mich nich sagen, wat det da oben uf det Dohr vorne Puppe is?« »Ja nu, wat wird det sinn! Alte römsche Geschichte. Kurfürsten von Brandenburg, siebenjährige Krieg, det is et!« »Aso! na ik danke recht sehr.«

The following lines render the original verses, written in Berlin dialect, in translation: "Can you tell me, my dear, what kind of a doll that is, up there on the Gate?" "Well, what could it possibly be? Ancient Roman history. Prince-Electors of Brandenburg, the Seven-Year-War, That's what it stands for." "I see! Well, thank ye."

30

31

Die vier Aquarelle von Friedrich August Calau aus der Zeit um 1820 zeigen den Blick vom Brandenburger Tor in den Tiergarten und umgekehrt (30, 31) sowie vom Tor auf die »Linden« und umgekehrt (32, 33).

The four water colours by Friedrich August Calau from around 1820 show the view from the Brandenburg Gate towards Tiergarten Park and vice versa (30, 31), as well as from the Gate towards the boulevard "Unter den Linden" and vice versa (32, 33).

32

33

Pariser Platz und Brandenburger Tor, Ölgemälde von Eduard Gaertner aus dem Jahre 1846.

Pariser Platz and Brandenburg Gate. Oil painting by Eduard Gaertner from 1846.

35

»Ansicht der Sommerschen Häuser zu Berlin«. Das um 1850 entstandene Ölgemälde von Theodor Rabe zeigt das Brandenburger Tor und seine Randbebauung vom Tiergarten aus.

"View of Sommer's Houses at Berlin". The oil painting by Theodor Rabe from around 1850 shows the Brandenburg Gate and neighbouring buildings as seen from Tiergarten Park.

36

37

Drei Siegesparaden: Der zeitgenössische Holzstich (36) zeigt den Einzug preußischer Truppen am 7. Dezember 1864 anläßlich des Sieges im deutsch-dänischen Krieg; die wohl erste Photographie des Brandenburger Tores (37) zeigt die Parade nach dem Sieg über Österreich am 20. September 1866; die beiden Hylographien (38, 39) zeigen den Einzug Kaiser Wilhelms I. in Berlin am 16. Juni 1871 zur Feier des Sieges im deutsch-französischen Krieg sowie die nächtlich Illumination des Brandenburger Tores aus diesem Anlaß.

Three victory parades: The contemporary wood engraving (36) shows the entry of Prussian troops on 7th December 1864 after victory in the German-Danish War; this, probably the first, photograph of the Brandenburg Gate (37) represents the parade after the victory over Austria on 20th September 1866; the two hylographs (38/39) depict the entry of Kaiser Wilhelm I into Berlin on 16th June 1871 for victory celebrations after the German-French War, as well as nocturnal illumination of the Brandenburg Gate at the same occasion.

38

39

Wilhelm I. bei der Ausfahrt in den Tiergarten (40). »Vale Senex Imperator« — Lebewohl, alter Kaiser, steht am Brandenburger Tor, als Wilhelm I. am 16. März 1888 zu Grabe getragen wird (41). »Dem Andenken des großen Kaisers« heißt das Gemälde von Ferdinand Keller (42).

Wilhelm I on his way to Tiergarten Park (40). "Vale Senex Imperator" — Farewell, Old Emperor, is written on the Brandenburg Gate when funeral services are held for Wilhelm I on 16th March 1888 (41)."To the Memory of the Great Kaiser" reads the title of the painting by Ferdinand Keller (42).

41

42

43

44

45

Die Zeichnung »An der Haltestelle« (43) stammt aus der Mappe »Spreeathener« von Christian Wilhelm Allers aus dem Jahre 1889. Die Nachtaufnahme (44) entstand am 2. September 1895 anläßlich der 25-Jahrfeier der Schlacht von Sedan. Aus etwa derselben Zeit ein Blick über den westlichen Vorplatz des Tores hin zum neuen Reichstagsgebäude (45).

"At the Tram Stop" (43), drawing from a series entitled "Spreeathener", which Christian Wilhelm Allers created in 1889. This nocturnal scene (44) was photographed on 2nd September 1895 during celebrations of the 25th anniversary of the battle of Sedan. The view across the western forecourt of the Gate towards the new "Reichstagsgebäude" (Parliament House) was taken at about the same time (45).

Der Pariser Platz an einem Apriltag 1896 (46). Die Quadriga wird von den Berlinern um die Jahrhundertwende »vierspännige Normaldroschke« genannt und als solche karikiert (47). Derlei Spott tat der Feierlichkeit jedoch keinen Abbruch: Einzug der Chinakrieger, die im Sommer 1900 gegen den sogenannten Boxeraufstand gekämpft hatten (48).

Pariser Platz on an April day in 1896 (46). By the turn of the century, Berliners had taken to calling the Quadriga a "four-horse hackney coach" and caricatured it as such (47). No ridicule though on solemn occasions: Return of the soldiers who, in the summer of 1900, had fought against the so-called Boxer Rebellion in China (48).

47

48

49

50

Stadtbaurat Hermann Blankenstein schlägt bereits in den sechziger Jahren des 19. Jahrhunderts eine Öffnung der Verbindung zwischen Portal und Seitenflügeln für den anwachsenden Verkehr vor (49). Sie wird ebensowenig verwirklicht wie die Vorschläge eines Wettbewerbs aus den Jahren 1907/1908: Zusätzliche Durchgänge durch seitliche Versetzung der Flügel, Urheber unbekannt (50); Abriß der Seitenbebauung von Ernst Eberhard v. Ihne (51); Tore durch die Seitenbebauung von Reimer & Körte (52); Freistellung des Tores von Ferdinand v. Strantz (53).

51

52

53

In the second half of the 19th century, Stadtbaurat (City Building Counsellor) Hermann Blankenstein already proposed eliminating the connection between the Gate and its side-wings to accommodate the increasing traffic (49). Neither this plan was realised, nor were the proposals resulting from a competition held in 1907/08, as e.g. this project by an unknown architect providing for the creation of additional passageways by a lateral shifting of the side-wings (50); demolition of the lateral buildings as proposed by Eberhard von Ihne (51); passageways through the lateral buildings as planned by Reimer & Körte (52); detachment of the Gate as projected by Ferdinand von Strantz (53).

54

55

56

Westansicht des Tores mit Schilderhäuschen, Aufnahme um 1905 (54). Aus dieser Zeit stammen auch die Aufnahmen von der Wache vor dem südlichen Torhaus (55) und von den Rollschuhfahrern im Tiergarten (56).

West view of the Gate with sentry boxes; photograph from around 1905 (54). These photographs of the guard in front of the southern Gate House (55), and of the roller skaters in Tiergarten Park (56) were taken at about the same time.

57

58

Kaiser Wilhelm II. (2.v.l.) 1911 beim Morgenritt in den Tiergarten (57). Zwei Jahre später, am 15. Juni 1913, findet ein festlicher Umzug zum 25jährigen Thronjubiläum des Monarchen statt (58). Bei diesem Anlaß kommt es zu einem Verkehrschaos am Brandenburger Tor (59).

Kaiser Wilhelm II (second from left) on his way to Tiergarten Park in 1911 (57). Two years later, on 15th June 1913, a festive procession takes place in celebration of the 25th anniversary of the monarch's accession to the throne (58). This occasion is also marked by a big traffic jam at the Brandenburg Gate (59).

1. August 1914: Ein Plakat an der Litfaßsäule verkündet die allgemeine Mobilmachung, der Erste Weltkrieg beginnt (60). Äußerlich bleibt es in Berlin vorerst friedlich, wie die Aufnahme aus dem Winter 1914/15 (61) und das Gemälde von Lesser Ury aus der Zeit um 1915 (62) zeigen.

1st August 1914: A bill proclaiming general mobilization: The First World War begins (60). At first, all remains peaceful in Berlin as this photograph, taken in the winter of 1914/15 (61), and Lesser Ury's painting from around 1915 (62) show.

62

63

64

65

Novemberrevolution 1918: Eine Volksmarine-Division marschiert in Berlin ein (63); der Arbeiter- und Soldatenrat patrouilliert am Brandenburger Tor (64); kommunistische Soldaten demonstrieren gegen die neue SPD-Regierung (65).

November-Revolution 1918: A division of the People's Marine marches into Berlin (63); members of the Workers' and Soldiers' Council patrolling the Brandenburg Gate (64); communist soldiers demonstrate against the new social-democrat government (65).

Am 10. Dezember 1918 kehrt die Garde mit klingendem Spiel von der Front nach Berlin zurück (66). Am 7. Januar 1919 besetzen Regierungstruppen im Kampf gegen Spartakisten das Brandenburger Tor (67, 68). Und am 3. März 1919 jubeln die Berliner Paul v. Lettow-Vorbeck und der heimkehrenden Schutztruppe aus Deutsch-Ostafrika zu (69).

68

69

On 10th December 1918, the guards regiment, with drums beating and trumpets sounding, returns from the front to Berlin (66). On 7th January 1919, Government troops fighting the left-wing Spartakists occupy the Brandenburg Gate (67, 68). And on 3rd March 1919, Berliners cheer Paul von Lettow-Vorbeck and his colonial forces upon their return from German East Africa (69).

70

71

März 1919: Freikorps-Werber ziehen durch die Stadt (70). Dezember 1919: Rückkehr der Baltikum-Kämpfer (71). 13. März 1920: Die Marinebrigade Ehrhardt zieht in Berlin ein (72) und besetzt das Brandenburger Tor (73); der Kapp-Putsch beginnt. 18. März 1920: Beim Rückzug schießen die gescheiterten Putschtruppen vor dem Tor in die Menge, zwölf Menschen kommen ums Leben (74).

March 1919: Recruiters for volunteer corps move through the city (70). December 1919: Return of the soldiers having fought in the Baltic States (71). 13th March 1920: The Marine Brigade Ehrhardt enters Berlin (72) and occupies the Brandenburg Gate (73); the (right-wing) Kapp-Putsch begins. 18th March 1920: Retreating putsch troops fire into the crowds gathered in front of the Gate; twelve people lose their lives (74).

72

73

74

1926 wird das Tor für Renovierungsarbeiten eingerüstet (75); zwei Jahre später wird die Wache am südlichen Torhaus entfernt (76). 1928 kehrt der »Eiserne Gustav« von seiner spektakulären Droschkentour nach Paris in seine Heimatstadt zurück (77).

In 1926, the Gate is scaffolded for renovation (75); two years later the guard facility at the southern Gate House is removed (76). In 1928, "Iron Gustav" returns to his native city after his spectacular hackney coach ride to Paris (77).

77

78

79

80

Am 10. Juni 1929 geleitet Reichspräsident Paul v. Hindenburg den ägyptischen König Fuad durch das Brandenburger Tor (78). Im Oktober desselben Jahres wird Gustav Stresemann zu Grabe getragen (79). Ebenfalls 1929 entsteht das Ölgemälde Ernst Ludwig Kirchners (80).

On 10th June 1929, Reich-President Paul von Hindenburg escorts Egyptian King Fuad through the Brandenburg Gate (78). In October of the same year, the funeral procession for Foreign Secretary Gustav Stresemann moves through the Gate (79). Ernst Ludwig Kirchner's oil painting (80) also dates from 1929.

81

Nie wieder ist der Langhans-Bau so oft gemalt worden wie in den zwanziger und frühen dreißiger Jahren unseres Jahrhunderts: Oskar Kokoschka, »Das Brandenburger Tor« (81); Hans Baluschek, »Unter den Linden 1930« (82); Felix Nussbaum, »Der tolle Platz« (83).

During the nineteen-twenties and early nineteen-thirties, the Gate frequently serves as subject for painters: Oskar Kokoschka, "The Brandenburg Gate" (81); Hans Baluschek, "Unter den Linden 1930" (82); Felix Nussbaum, "The Mad Square" (83).

83

82

85

86

»Jeder einmal in Berlin« — das Tor als Kulisse für ein Erinnerungsphoto (85) und für eine Wahlkampagne (86). Die Luftaufnahme (84) stammt aus der Mitte der dreißiger Jahre.

"On a visit to Berlin" — the Gate as backdrop for a souvenir photograph (85) and for an election campaign (86). The aerial photograph was taken in the mid-nineteen-thirties (84).

117

87

88

Der Fackelzug der Nationalsozialisten am Abend des 30. Januar 1933, dem Tag, als Hitler in die Reichskanzlei einzieht (87), und die (besser ausgeleuchtete) Neuinszenierung dieses Ereignisses für einen NS-Propagandafilm im Sommer desselben Jahres (88). Eine erschreckend hellsichtige Vision des Kommenden ist die Zeichnung von Theo Matejko aus dem Jahre 1933 (89).

The Nazi torch parade on the evening of 30th January 1933, the day Hitler became Chancellor of the Reich (87), and the (better lighted) restaging of the event in the summer of the same year for a Nazi propaganda movie (88). There can hardly be a more striking premonition of things to come than the one expressed in this drawing by Theo Matejko from the year 1933 (89).

90

91

Das brennende Reichstagsgebäude am 28. Februar 1933 (90). Die Titelseite der »Berliner Illustrirten« zeigt den Fackelzug zum »Tag von Potsdam« am 21. März 1933 (91). Festzug der Berliner Innungen anläßlich der Reichshandwerkswoche am 22. Oktober 1933 (92, 93).

The burning Reichstag (Parliament House) on 28th February 1933 (90). The cover of the "Berliner Illustrirte" shows the torch parade on the "Day of Potsdam" on 21st March 1933 (91). Pageant of Berlin Guilds on 22nd October 1933 on the occasion of the "Reichshandwerkswoche" (Week of the Arts and Crafts) (92, 93).

92

93

94

95

Das Brandenburger Tor als Standardkulisse: Im Juni 1934 besucht die »Alte Garde« der Hamburger SA Berlin (94); am 19. August 1934 wird die Übernahme der Befugnisse des Reichspräsidenten durch Adolf Hitler gefeiert (95).

Folgende Doppelseite:
Die Westseite des Brandenburger Tores in den dreißiger Jahren (96). Hier ereignet sich am 20. August 1935 beim Bau eines S-Bahn-Tunnels eine Einsturzkatastrophe, der neunzehn Arbeiter zum Opfer fallen (97).
Schadows Quadriga schmückt das offizielle Plakat für die 11. Olympischen Sommerspiele, die vom 1. bis 16. August 1936 in Berlin stattfinden (98).

The Brandenburg Gate as a favourite backdrop: In June 1934, the "Old Guard" of the Hamburg SA (a Nazi party formation) visits Berlin (94); on 19th August 1934, the conferment of presidential powers upon Adolf Hitler is celebrated (95).

Following pages:
The west side of the Brandenburg Gate in the nineteen-thirties (96). It was here that an accident occurred on 20th August 1935 at the construction site of a local railway tunnel, costing the lives of nineteen workers (97).
Schadow's Quadriga adorns the official poster for the 11th Olympic Summer Games which took place in Berlin from 1st to 16th August 1936 (98).

96

97

99

100

Zu den zahlreichen Attraktionen der Olympischen Spiele gehört auch ein Besuch des Zeppelins LZ 129 »Hindenburg« (99). Getränkeverkäufer vor dem geschmückten Brandenburger Tor (100). Olympischer Festschmuck am Pariser Platz (101).

Among the numerous attractions of the Olympic Games was a visit of Zeppelin LZ 129, named "Hindenburg" (99). Vendors of beverages in front of the decorated Brandenburg Gate (100). "Olympic" decorations at the Pariser Platz (101).

101

102

103

Im August 1937 findet die 700-Jahrfeier Berlins statt. Scharen von Berlinern sind auf den Beinen (102), um den großen Festumzug zu sehen. Blick vom Dach des Brandenburger Tores (103).

In August 1937, Berlin celebrates its 700th anniversary. Large crowds of Berliners are up and about to see the big parade (102). View from the roof of the Brandenburg Gate (103).

104

Der Langhans-Bau als Hintergrund für eine Rollschlittschuhvorführung (104). Als der italienische Diktator Benito Mussolini im September 1937 Berlin besucht, wird die Straße Unter den Linden zu einer Via Triumphalis umgestaltet. Links unten auf der Aufnahme ist die Wagenkolonne des »Duce« zu sehen (105).

The Brandenburg Gate as background for a performance of skaters (104). When Italian Dictator Benito Mussolini visited Berlin in September 1937, the boulevard "Unter den Linden" was turned into a triumphal way. On the lower left of the photograph the automobile convoy of the "Duce" is visible (105).

105

106

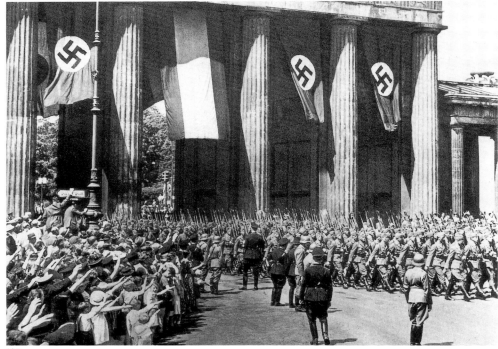

107

Berlins Feierlichkeiten sind Ende der dreißiger Jahre zunehmend militärisch geprägt: Empfang des ungarischen Reichsverwesers Admiral Nikolaus Horthy durch Hitler am 24. August 1938 (106); Heimkehr der Legion Condor, die im Spanischen Bürgerkrieg an der Seite Francos gekämpft hat (107); Lichtdom zur Feier des Anschlusses des Sudetengebiets am 1. Oktober 1938 (108); Hitler auf dem Weg zur Militärparade anläßlich seines fünfzigsten Geburtstages am 20. April 1939 (109).

By the end of the nineteen-thirties, Berlin's manifestations of state increasingly take on a predominantly military aspect: Reception of the Hungarian "Reichsverweser" (Reich Administrator) Admiral Nikolaus Horthy by Hitler on 24th August 1938 (106); return of the "Legion Condor" which had fought on the side of Franco in the Spanish Civil War (107); "Dome of Light" in celebration of the "Anschluß" (annexation) of the Sudetenland on 1st October 1938 (108); Hitler on his way to the military parade in honour of his 50th birthday on 20th April 1939 (109).

108

109

110

111

Aus Berlin sollte nach Hitlers Vorstellungen die Welthauptstadt »Germania« werden. Einen Eindruck von den gigantischen Umbauplänen, die Albert Speer entworfen hat, geben die hier abgebildeten Modelle (110, 111). Hans Stephan, Abteilungsleiter in der zuständigen Planungsbehörde, karikierte 1941 die Maßlosigkeit der Bauvorhaben (112).

It was Hitler's intention to make of Berlin the World Capital "Germania". The scale models shown here (110, 111) give an impression of the gigantic development plans Albert Speer had designed. Hans Stephan, then Department Head of the Planning Authority in charge, caricatured the excessive grandeur of the construction projects (112).

112

113

114

115

Am 18. Juli 1940 wird am Brandenburger Tor eine Tribüne errichtet (113), von der herab Propagandaminister Joseph Goebbels und General der Artillerie Friedrich Fromm eine vom Frankreich-Feldzug zurückkehrende siegreiche Infanteriedivision begrüßen (114). Tausende Berliner bilden Spalier (115).

On 18th July 1940, a platform is erected at the Brandenburg Gate (113) from which Propaganda Minister Joseph Goebbels and General of the Artillery Friedrich Fromm are welcoming an infantry division returning from the victorious campaign against France (114). Thousands of Berliners are forming a lane of spectators (115).

116

12. November 1940: Der sowjetische Außenminister Molotow auf dem Weg zu Verhandlungen mit Hitler über die beiderseitigen Interessensphären (116).
Am 24. März 1941 wird der berühmte Eisenbahnwaggon von Compiègne, in dem Deutschland 1918 kapituliert und Frankreich 1940 Hitlers Waffenstillstandsbedingungen entgegengenommen hat, in den Berliner Lustgarten transportiert (117).

12th November 1940: Soviet Foreign Secretary Molotov on his way to Hitler for negotiations concerning the respective spheres of interest (116). On 24th March 1941, the famous railway carriage from the French town of Compiègne, in which German capitulation had been signed in 1918, and, in 1940, France had accepted Hitler's armistice conditions, was transferred to the Berlin Lustgarten Park (117).

117

118

Der Bombenkrieg erreicht die Reichshauptstadt. Um feindlichen Fliegern die Orientierung zu erschweren, wird die Ost-West-Achse im Tiergarten mit Tarnnetzen verhängt (118). Während des Endkampfes um Berlin 1945 wird das Brandenburger Tor verbarrikadiert (119), wie es der britische Karikaturist David Low bereits Jahre zuvor vorausgesehen hat (120).

The bombing raids have attained the capital of the Reich. To deter enemy planes, the avenue "Ost-West-Achse" in Tiergarten Park is hung with camouflage netting (118). The Brandenburg Gate is barricaded for the final battle of Berlin in 1945 (119), exactly as it had been envisioned years before by British caricaturist David Low (120).

119

120

121

122

123

Das Ende. Am 1. Mai hissen sowjetische Soldaten auf der völlig zerschossenen Quadriga die rote Sowjetflagge (121). Die Umgebung des Tores bietet ein Bild der Verwüstung (122). Vor dieser gespenstischen Kulisse hält der russische Schriftsteller Jewgeni Dolmatowski eine Rede an die Soldaten der Roten Armee (123).

The end. On 1st May 1945, Soviet soldiers hoist the red flag on the severely damaged Quadriga (121). The area surrounding the Gate presents a picture of devastation (122). Before this macabre backdrop Russian author Yevgeniy Dolmatovsky addresses the soldiers of the Red Army (123).

124

125

Im Mai 1945 hält die Rote Armee vor dem Brandenburger Tor ihre Siegesparade ab (124); die russische Inschrift am Tor lautet: »Ruhm den sowjetischen Streitkräften, die das Banner des Sieges über Berlin gehißt haben« (125). Flüchtlinge in den Tor-Ruinen (126).
Einrücken der US-Truppen in Berlin im Juli 1945 (127).

In May 1945, the Red Army holds its victory parade before the Brandenburg Gate (124); the Russian language inscription on the Gate says: "Glory to the Soviet Armed Forces Who Have Raised the Banner of Victory Over Berlin" (125). Refugees camping in the ruins of the Gate (126).
U.S. troops entering Berlin in July 1945 (127).

126

127

128

Die Überreste des Langhans-Baus im Sommer 1945 (128). Inmitten der Trümmerwüste regt sich schon bald wieder Leben (129). Razzia auf dem Schwarzmarkt am Brandenburger Tor (130).

Remains of the Brandenburg Gate in the summer of 1945 (128). New life is beginning to bud in a wasteland of rubble (129). Raid on the black market at the Brandenburg Gate (130).

129

130

131

132

Ein unbeschrankter Bahnübergang mitten Unter den Linden: Trümmerlok 1946 (131). Torschmuck zum 1. Mai 1946 (132). Die traurigen Reste der Minerva-Statue mit Wahlplakaten der SED im Oktober 1947 (133).

A railway track crossing the boulevard "Unter den Linden" with a so-called "Trümmerlok" (locomotive removing rubble) in 1946 (131). The Gate decorated for May Day 1946 (132). The sad remains of the Minerva statue covered with SED-election posters in October 1947 (133).

133

Not macht erfinderisch: Der Tiergarten ist gerodet worden, um dringend benötigte Nahrungsmittel anzubauen.

Necessity is the mother of invention: Tiergarten Park has been cleared of trees so that it can be used for the cultivation of urgently needed vegetables and potatoes.

135

137

Deutschlandtreffen der sozialistischen »Freien deutschen Jugend« (FDJ) im Mai 1950 in Berlin (135). Trümmerfrauen vor dem Brandenburger Tor (136). Halbmastbeflaggung zu Stalins Tod am 6. März 1953 (137).

Meeting of the socialist "Freie Deutsche Jugend" (Free German Youth) in May 1950 in Berlin (135). Berlin's famous "Trümmerfrauen" (Rubble Women) (136). The red flag at half mast upon Stalin's death on 6th March 1953 (137).

136

Volksaufstand am 17. Juni 1953: Die verhaßte rote Fahne wird vom Brandenburger Tor geholt und von Demonstranten verbrannt (138–140).

People's uprising on 17th June 1953. Demonstrators remove the detested red flag from the Brandenburg Gate and burn it (138–140).

138

139

140

Am 17. Juni 1953 ziehen Demonstranten, das Deutschlandlied singend, mit schwarz-rot-goldenen Fahnen in den Westteil der Stadt.

On 17th June 1953, demonstrators with German national flags march into the western part of the city, singing the German national anthem.

Folgende Doppelseite:
Die Aufnahme des Fotografen Fritz Eschen wirkt wie ein Symbol für den kalten Krieg, unter dem Berlin in den fünfziger Jahren besonders leidet (142).
Am 2. Februar 1957 stattet Bundeskanzler Konrad Adenauer Berlin einen seiner wenigen Besuche ab. Der Regierende Bürgermeister Otto Suhr geleitet ihn zum Brandenburger Tor (143).

Following pages:
Photographer Fritz Eschen's picture appears like a symbol for the Cold War in the nineteen-fifties, during which Berlin in particular suffered considerably (142). On 2nd February 1957, Chancellor Konrad Adenauer comes to Berlin for one of his rare visits. Governing Mayor Otto Suhr escorts him to the Brandenburg Gate (143).

142

143

144

1957 läßt der Ost-Berliner Magistrat den Langhans-Bau restaurieren (144). Das Richtfest am 14. Dezember 1957 nutzt der stellvertretende Oberbürgermeister Waldemar Schmidt zu Propaganda-Attacken auf den West-Berliner Senat (145).

In 1957 the East Berlin Magistrate has the Brandenburg Gate restored (144). The topping-out ceremony on 14th December 1957 is used by Vice-Mayor Waldemar Schmidt to launch propaganda attacks on the West Berlin Senate (145).

145

146

Nach vorhandenen Gipsformen und genauen Vermessungen des Amts für Denkmalpflege fertigt die West-Berliner Bildgießerei Noack in den Jahren 1957/1958 eine originalgetreue Nachbildung der Quadriga (146–149).

Using surviving casting moulds and measurements from the Office of Preservation of Ancient Monuments, the West Berlin foundry Noack in 1957/58 creates an exact replica of the Quadriga (146–149).

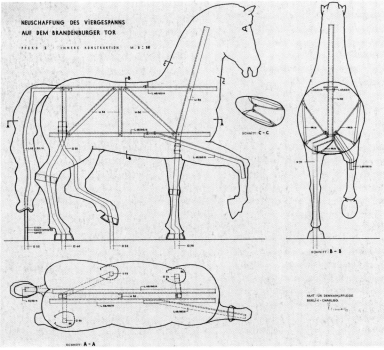

147

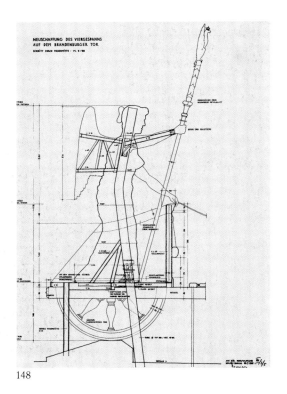

148

149

150

151

152

153

164

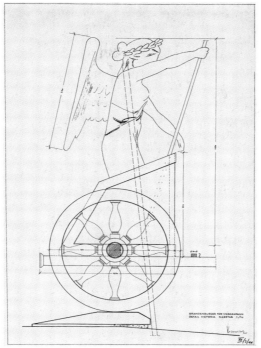
154

155

156

Der preußische Adler und das Eiserne Kreuz, die die Panierstange der Siegesgöttin schmücken, müssen frei nachgestaltet werden, weil von ihnen keine Gipsformen mehr existieren (150–153). Die Wagenräder haben einen Durchmesser von rund 2,5 Metern (154, 155). Ende Juli 1958 kann Hermann Noack (links) Bürgermeister Franz Amrehn vom Abschluß der Arbeiten unterrichten (156).

The Prussian Eagle and the Iron Cross adorning the staff of the Goddess of Victory have to be fashioned "from memory" as for them no casting moulds exist (150–153). The wheels of the chariot have a diametre of ca. 2,5 metres (154, 155). At the end of July 1958, Hermann Noack (left) informs Mayor Franz Amrehn of the completion of the work (156).

Am 1. August 1958 verläßt die neugeschaffene Siegesgöttin West-Berlin...

On 1st August 1958 a re-born Goddess of Victory leaves West Berlin...

158

159

Auf dem Pariser Platz wird Schadows Viergespann provisorisch zusammengesetzt und von den Berlinern willkommen geheißen (158). Selbst Ost-Berlins Oberbürgermeister Friedrich Ebert jun. (rechts) und sein Stellvertreter Waldemar Schmidt lassen sich vor der Quadriga ablichten; jedoch hat man für dieses Foto die Trophäen der Göttin verhängt (160). Eisernes Kreuz und Preußen-Adler sind der kommunistischen Stadtführung nicht mehr opportun. Vorschläge für linientreue Alternativen (159). Der Siegeswagen wird zunächst in den Hof des Marstalls verbracht (161).

On Pariser Platz, Schadow's Quadriga is provisionally assembled and welcomed by the Berlin population (158). Even East Berlin Mayor Friedrich Ebert jun. (right) and his Deputy Waldemar Schmidt pose for photographs with the Quadriga, but only after the emblems of the Goddess have been covered by a cloth (160). Iron Cross and Prussian Eagle are unacceptable to the communist city administration; appropriate alternatives are already under consideration (159). For the present, the victory chariot is taken to the courtyard of the Marstall (Royal Stables) (161).

Folgende Doppelseite:
Im September 1958 kehrt die Quadriga — ohne Eisernes Kreuz und preußischen Adler — an ihren angestammten Platz zurück (162, 163).

Following pages:
In September 1958, the Quadriga — without Iron Cross and Prussian Eagle — returns to its accustomed place (162, 163).

160

161

163

Phototermine am wiederhergestellten Tor: US-Senator Hubert H. Humphrey und der Regierende Bürgermeister Willy Brandt, November 1958 (164); die Schöneberger Sängerknaben, Weihnachten 1959 (165); sowjetische Soldaten (166); Billy Wilder, Pamela Tiffin, James Cagney und Horst Buchholz (von links) während der Dreharbeiten für »Eins, zwei, drei« im August 1961, unmittelbar vor dem Mauerbau (167).

Posing for pictures at the restored Gate: U.S. Senator Hubert H. Humphrey and Governing Mayor Willy Brandt, November 1958 (164); The Schöneberg Choir Boys, Christmas 1959 (165); Soviet soldiers (166); Billy Wilder, Pamela Tiffin, James Cagney and Horst Buchholz (from left to right) during filming of "Eins, zwei, drei", August 1961, right before erection of the wall (167).

166

167

13. August 1961: Das Brandenburger Tor wird abgeriegelt. Der Bau der Mauer beginnt.

13th August 1961: The Brandenburg Gate ist closed off. The erection of the wall begins.

169

170

Brutale Realität und propagandistische Verarbeitung: Kampfgruppenmitglieder, die das Tor abriegeln, und ihre Heroisierung auf einem Schulbuchumschlag (169, 170). Ernest G. Reuter läßt auf seiner Lithographie von 1961 ein Mädchen mit wippendem Petticoat durch die aufmarschierten »Verteidiger des Arbeiter- und Bauernstaates« tänzeln (171). Gepanzerte Fahrzeuge blockieren die Tordurchfahrten (172).

Harsh reality and its propagandistic transformation: Members of East German "Kampfgruppen" (Combat Groups) barring the Gate, and their later glorification on a schoolbook cover (169/170). In his 1961 lithograph, Ernest G. Reuter has a girl with rustling petticoats dance through the lines of "Defenders of the Workers' and Peasants' State" (171), as the East German regime calls itself. Armoured cars block the Gate passages (172).

171

172

173

174

175

176

Szenen vom August 1961. Im Osten Soldaten der Nationalen Volksarmee und Angehörige der Betriebskampfgruppen der DDR, die entschlossen einen unmenschlichen Befehl ausführen (173–175). Im Westen Politiker und Militärs, denen die Ratlosigkeit ins Gesicht geschrieben steht: Bundestagspräsident Eugen Gerstenmaier auf dem Dach des Reichstagsgebäudes (176); Willy Brandt mit US-General Bruce C. Clarke (177).

Scenes from August 1961. On the east side of the wall, soldiers of the National People's Army and GDR Combat Groups executing an inhuman order (173–175). On the west side, politicians and members of the military, their faces expressing complete perplexity: Bundestagspräsident (President of Parliament) Eugen Gerstenmaier on the roof of the Reichstagsgebäude (Parliament House) (176); Willy Brandt with U.S. General Bruce C. Clarke (177).

177

178

179

Bundesminister Ernst Lemmer informiert sich über die Situation am Brandenburger Tor (178).
Geradezu unheimlich wirkt die äußerliche Gelassenheit, mit der die Zaungäste am Morgen des 13. August die Sperrmaßnahmen beobachten (179).
Im November 1961 wird im Halbrund vor dem Tor eine massive Panzersperre errichtet (180).

West German Minister Ernst Lemmer receiving firsthand information on the situation at the Brandenburg Gate (178). There is something uncanny in the outward calm with which onlookers observe the barring measures on the morning of 13th August 1961 (179).
In November 1961, a massive anti-tank barrier is built in a semi-circle in front of the Gate (180).

Das abgeriegelte Tor im Grenzgebiet zwischen Ost und West.

The closed-off Gate at the frontier between East and West.

182

183

Als John F. Kennedy am 26. Juni 1963 das Brandenburger Tor besucht, hat die DDR-Regierung die Durchfahrten verhängt. Dem mächtigen US-Präsidenten sollen seine Grenzen demonstriert werden (182). Am 27. Mai 1965 besucht die britische Königin Elizabeth II. das Tor (183). Den weiteren Ausbau der Mauer im Jahr 1966 kommentiert Ost-Berlin mit unglaublichem Zynismus selbst (184).

When John F. Kennedy visits the Brandenburg Gate on 26th June 1963, the GDR-Government has the view through the Gate blocked by cloth panels to show the mighty U.S. President that even his power is limited (182).
On 27th May 1965 Queen Elizabeth II visits the Gate (183). East Berlin comments with unique cynicism on reenforcement of the wall (184). The billboard bears the following warning "Trying to Force the State Border or Engaging in Provocative Action at the Wall Will Only Make Matters Worse!"

184

Auch das eingemauerte Tor bleibt vielen Künstlern Anregung für ihre Arbeit: Wolf Vostell, »Mauer, Brandenburger Tor, Häuser«, Photographie und Beton, 1972 (185); Harald Metzkes, »Brandenburger Tor«, Öl auf Leinwand, 1978 (186).

Even walled up the Gate serves as inspiration for numerous artists: Wolf Vostell, "Wall, Brandenburg Gate, Houses", Photograph and concrete, 1972 (185); Harald Metzkes, "The Brandenburg Gate", Oil on canvas, 1978 (186).

187

188

Protestaktionen wie die zum 25. Jahrestag des Mauerbaus am 13. August 1986 werden immer seltener (187, 188). Doch als Kulisse für Großveranstaltungen wie den Berlin-Marathon (189) und als Touristenattraktion – hier auf Ost-Berliner Seite (190) – ist das Tor beliebt wie eh und je.

Protest demonstrations like the one on 13th August 1986, the 25th anniversary of the erection of the wall, are getting rare (187/188). But as a backdrop for mass events such as the Berlin Marathon (189), and as a tourist attraction — here the East Berlin side (190) — the Gate is a favourite as ever before.

189

190

Folgende Doppelseite:
Eine politische Wende bahnt sich an. Am 16. April 1986 besucht Generalsekretär Michail Gorbatschow mit Ehefrau Raissa Ost-Berlin (191). Und am 12. Juni 1987 fordert US-Präsident Ronald Reagan in einer Rede vor dem Brandenburger Tor den KPdSU-Chef auf, die Mauer niederzureißen (192).

Following pages:
A political turn-about in the offing. On 16th April 1986, General Secretary Mikhail Gorbachev and his wife Raissa visit East Berlin (191). And in a speech at the Brandenburg Gate on 12th June 1987, U.S. President Ronald Reagan appeals to the head of the Soviet communist party to tear down the wall (192).

191

190

Das Unfaßbare wird wahr: In der Nacht vom 9. zum 10. November 1989 öffnen sich die Grenzen der DDR und Ost-Berlins. Ein Extrablatt der BILD-Zeitung verkündet: »Geschafft! Die Mauer ist offen« (193). Noch in der Nacht und den ganzen folgenden Tag über feiern und tanzen die Berliner auf der Mauer vor dem Brandenburger Tor (194, 195).

A dream comes true. In the night of 9th November 1989, GDR and East Berlin borders are opened. A special edition of the BILD-Zeitung announces: "It's Done! The Wall Is Open!" (193). All through that night and the following day Berliners celebrate and dance on top of the wall at the Brandenburg Gate (194, 195).

193

194

195

196

197

Am 10. November ist die Mauer vor dem Brandenburger Tor noch fest in der Hand der Berliner (196); am 11. November marschieren ein letztes Mal DDR-Grenztruppen auf (197). In den folgenden Tagen und Wochen finden sich Medienvertreter aus aller Welt und Hunderte von Schaulustigen vor dem Tor ein, um bei der Öffnung der Mauer an diesem symbolischen Ort dabeizusein (198, 199).

On 10th November, the wall at the Brandenburg Gate is still "occupied" by Berliners (196); on 11th November, GDR Border Troops march up for the last time (197). During the following days and weeks reporting teams from all over the world and hundreds of spectators gather at the Gate to witness the opening of the wall at this special place (198, 199).

198

199

Am 22. Dezember 1989 wird die Mauer am Brandenburger Tor geöffnet. Bei strömendem Regen versammeln sich Tausende von Berlinern und viel Prominenz, um das große Ereignis mitzuerleben.
Von rechts: Bundesaußenminister Hans-Dietrich Genscher, Altbundespräsident Walter Scheel, Bundeskanzler Helmut Kohl, Regierender Bürgermeister Walter Momper, DDR-Ministerpräsident Hans Modrow, Kanzleramtsminister Rudolf Seiters und DDR-Außenminister Oskar Fischer.

On 22nd December 1989, the wall at the Brandenburg Gate opens. Thousands of Berliners and many VIP's gather in pouring rain to witness this great event. From the right: Foreign Secretary Hans-Dietrich Genscher, former Federal President Walter Scheel, Chancellor Helmut Kohl, West Berlin's Governing Mayor Walter Momper, GDR Prime Minister Hans Modrow, Chancellery Minister Rudolf Seiters and GDR Foreign Secretary Oskar Fischer.

201

Das Tor am Tag seiner Öffnung, dem 22. Dezember 1989.

The Gate on the day of its opening, the 22nd December 1989.

203

Berlin, Brandenburger Tor,
1. Januar 1990, 00:00 Uhr.

Berlin, the Brandenburg Gate,
1st January 1990, 00:00 hours.

204

Januar 1990: Am neuen Übergang Brandenburger Tor bilden sich täglich lange Menschenschlangen (204). Die Silvesterfeier hat den Torbau und die Quadriga stark in Mitleidenschaft gezogen. Die Siegesgöttin ist mit Graffiti übersät (205). Im März 1990 wird das Tor eingerüstet und das Viergespann zur Restaurierung abmontiert. Im April schließlich fällt die Mauer an diesem symbolträchtigen Ort endgültig (206, 207).

January 1990: Day by day, long lines of people form at the new opening at the Brandenburg Gate (204). The celebration of New Year's Eve left the Gate and the Quadriga much the worse for it. The Goddess of Victory is covered by graffiti (205). In March 1990 scaffolding is set up all around the Gate, and the Quadriga is taken down for repairs. In April the wall at this historic site comes down at last (206, 207).

205

206

207

208

Danksagung
Acknowledgments

Der Autor möchte all denen, die ihm mit Rat und Hilfe zur Seite gestanden haben, herzlich danken: dem Verlag Ullstein und Christian Seeger als Lektor, der die Veröffentlichung mit größtem Engagement gefördert hat, Hild Wollenhaupt für die einfühlsame Übersetzung ins Englische, Wolfgang Gottschalk vom Märkischen Museum, der stets ansprechbar war und wertvolle Hinweise gab, Helmut Reichardt, der die Arbeit mit großem Wohlwollen gefördert hat, sowie zahlreichen Privatpersonen und Institutionen, die hier nicht alle einzeln aufgezählt werden können. Schließlich danke ich meiner Frau Gabriele, die mir während der Zeit des Lesens, Sammelns und Schreibens – wie schon so oft – den Rücken frei gehalten hat, so daß aus einer ersten Idee die vorliegende Veröffentlichung werden konnte.

The author wishes to express his gratitude to all those who have assisted him with advice and practical help in this undertaking: To Ullstein Verlag and editor Christian Seeger, who so encouragingly supported the work; to Hild Wollenhaupt for her sensitive translation into English; to Wolfgang Gottschalk of the Märkische Museum, unfailing in his readiness to make valuable suggestions, as well as to numerous individuals and institutions which it is impossible to name here. Last but not least, I wish to thank my wife, Gabriele, who, as so often before provided an environment conducive to the process of reading, gathering material and writing so that an initial idea could develop into the publication at hand.

Ausgewählte Literatur
Selected Bibliography

ARCHITEKTEN-VEREIN ZU BERLIN (HG.).): Berlin und seine Bauten, Berlin 1877.

BACKES, UWE u. a.: Reichstagsbrand. Aufklärung einer historischen Legende, München 1986.
BAUCH, KURT: Das Brandenburger Tor, Berlin 1968.
BLOCH, PETER u. GRZIMEK, WALDEMAR: Das klassische Berlin. Die Berliner Bildhauerschule im neunzehnten Jahrhundert, Frankfurt/Main 1978.
BÖRSCH-SUPAN, HELMUT: Die Kataloge der Berliner Akademie-Ausstellungen 1786–1850, Berlin 1971.

DANKE, RUDOLF: »In diesem Hause wohnte Max Liebermann«, in: Der Bär von Berlin, Jahrbuch des Vereins für die Geschichte Berlins, 15. Folge, Berlin 1966.
DEHIO, GEORG u. a.: Handbuch der deutschen Kunstdenkmäler Berlin/DDR, Postdam, München 1983.
DETTBARN-REGGENTIN, JÜRGEN: »Der Tiergarten«, in: Orgel-Köhne, Liselotte u. Armin: Der Tiergarten Berlin. Geschichte und Gegenwart, o. O. 1985.

ECKARDT, GÖTZ (HG.): Schicksale deutscher Baudenkmale im zweiten Weltkrieg. Eine Dokumentation der Schäden und Totalverluste auf dem Gebiet der Deutschen Demokratischen Republik, München 1978.
ENGEL, HELMUT U. A. (HG.): Tiergarten. Teil 1 – Vom Brandenburger Tor zum Zoo, Berlin 1989.

FONTANE, THEODOR: Der deutsche Krieg von 1866, Berlin 1871.
FONTANE, THEODOR: Gedichte, in: Werke, Schriften und Briefe Abt. I, Bd. 6, München 1964.
Freiheit – schöner Götterfunken. Die glücklichen Tage von Berlin, Frankfurt/Main, Berlin 1990.

Grieben-Reiseführer, Berlin und Umgebung, Berlin 1936.

HERTSLET, WILLIAM LEWIS u. HOFMANN, WINFRIED: Der Treppenwitz der Weltgeschichte. Geschichtliche Irrtümer, Entstellungen und Erfindungen, Frankfurt/Main, Berlin 1984.

Herzogin Viktoria Luise: Ein Leben als Tochter des Kaisers, Olten 1965.
Hildebrandt, Rainer: Es geschah an der Mauer, Berlin 1966.
Hildebrandt, Rainer: Der 17. Juni, Berlin 1983.
Hoffmann, E.T.A.: Ritter Gluck, in: Poetische Werke Bd. 1, Berlin 1957.
Hohenlohe-Ingelfingen, Prinz Kraft zu: Aus meinem Leben, Berlin 1897–1907.

Institut für Denkmalpflege der DDR (Hg.): Die Bau- und Kunstdenkmale in der DDR. Hauptstadt Berlin I, München 1983.

Katalog Berlin Museum: Stadtbilder. Berlin in der Malerei vom 17. Jahrhundert bis zur Gegenwart, Berlin 1987.
Katalog Landesarchiv Berlin: Von Berlin nach Germania. Über die Zerstörung der »Reichshauptstadt« durch Albert Speers Neugestaltungsplanungen, Berlin 1984.
Kindler, Helmut: Berlin Brandenburger Tor. Brennpunkt deutscher Geschichte, München 1956.
Klünner, Hans-Werner: S- und U-Bahnarchitektur in Berlin, Berlin 1985.
Koch, Hannsjoachim W.: Der deutsche Bürgerkrieg. Eine Geschichte der deutschen und österreichischen Freikorps 1918–1923, Frankfurt/Main, Berlin 1978.
Krieger, Bogdan: Berlin im Wandel der Zeiten. Eine Wanderung vom Schloß nach Charlottenburg durch 3 Jahrhunderte, Berlin-Grunewald 1923.
Kurowski, Franz: Bedingungslose Kapitulation. Inferno in Deutschland 1945, Leoni am Starnberger See 1983.

Lachmann, Rainer: »Die Quadriga auf dem Brandenburger Tor, insbes. das Einsetzen des Eisernen Kreuzes im Siegeskranz. Aus wiedergefundenem Original-Brief Karl Friedrich Schinkels mit Datum: ›Berlin 26ten Mai 1814‹«, in: Der Herold. Vierteljahrsschrift für Heraldik, Genealogie und verwandte Wissenschaften, N. F. Band 13, Heft 1, Berlin 1990.
Laverrenz, Victor: Die Denkmäler Berlins und der Volkswitz, Berlin 1900.
Löschburg, Winfried: Unter den Linden. Gesichter und Geschichten einer berühmten Straße, Berlin 1972.

Mackowsky, Hans: Häuser und Menschen im alten Berlin, Berlin 1923.
Montez, Lola (Gräfin v. Landsfeld): Memoiren, Frankfurt/Main 1986.

Nicolai, Friedrich: Beschreibung der königlichen Residenzstadt Berlin (1786). Eine Auswahl, Berlin 1987.

Ribbe, Wolfgang (Hg.): Geschichte Berlins, München 1987.
Romberg, J.H.F. (Hg.): Die Stimme der Wahrheit aus dem göttlichen Worte. Über Friedrich Wilhelm III. König von Preußen, Berlin 1842.

Schadow, Johann Gottfried: Kunstwerke und Kunstansichten. Ein Quellenwerk zur Berliner Kunst- und Kulturgeschichte zwischen 1780 und 1845. Kommentierte Neuausgabe der Veröffentlichung von 1849, herausgegeben von Götz Eckardt, Berlin 1987.
Scharf, Helmut: Kleine Kunstgeschichte des deutschen Denkmals, Darmstadt 1984.
Schmidt, Hartwig: »Carl Gotthard Langhans«, in: Ribbe, Wolfgang u. Schäche, Wolfgang: Baumeister, Architekten, Stadtplaner. Biographien zur baulichen Entwicklung Berlins, Berlin 1987.
Scholz, Hans: »Deutschlands Portal. Das Brandenburger Tor (1791)«, in: Koch, Hans Jürgen (Hg.): Wallfahrtsstätten der Nation. Zwischen Brandenburg und Bayern, Frankfurt/Main 1986.
Siefart, Emil v.: »Aus der Geschichte des Brandenburger Tores und der Quadriga«, in: Schriften des Vereins für die Geschichte Berlins, Heft XLV, Berlin 1912.
Speer, Albert: Architektur. Arbeiten 1933–1942, Frankfurt/Main, Berlin 1978.
Speier, Hans-Michael: Berlin! Berlin! Eine Großstadt im Gedicht, Stuttgart 1987.
Staël, Anne Germaine de: Über Deutschland, herausgegeben von Monika Bosse nach der deutschen Erstausgabe 1814, Frankfurt/Main 1985.

Velin, Regulus: »Der Baumeister des Brandenburger Tores. Historiographisches über den Architekten Carl Gotthard Langhans«, in: Berliner Forum 5/83, Berlin 1983.
Venner, Dominique: Söldner ohne Sold. Die deutschen Freikorps 1918–1923, Wien 1974.
Voss, Karl: Reiseführer für Literaturfreunde: Berlin. Vom Alex bis zum Kudamm, Frankfurt/Main 1980.

Woche, Klaus-Rainer: Vom Wecken bis zum Zapfenstreich. Vier Jahrhunderte Garnison Berlin, Berg am See 1986.
Wolf, Gerhard (Hg.): Rückwärts gehn die Krebse gern, vorwärts eilt die Zeit. Berliner Biedermeier in Vers und Prosa, Berlin 1988.

Zedlitz, Leopold Frhr. v.: Neuestes Conversations-Handbuch über Berlin und Postdam zum täglichen Gebrauch der Einheimischen und Fremden aller Stände, Berlin 1834 (ND Leipzig 1987).

Archivalien des Ullstein Textarchivs.

Bildnachweis
Illustration Credits

ADN-Zentralbild, Berlin: 191
Berlinische Galerie, Berlin: 83
Berlin-Museum, Berlin, mit freundlicher Genehmigung der
VG Bild-Kunst, Bonn: 185, 186
Bildarchiv Preußischer Kulturbesitz, Berlin: 20, 36, 80
Deutsche Presse-Agentur, Frankfurt/M: 200
Archiv Wolfgang Gottschalk, Berlin: 170
Landesbildstelle Berlin: 1, 2, 6—11, 14, 16, 26, 27, 40, 45, 46, 61,
81, 85, 96, 100, 101, 117, 119, 120, 122, 126, 129, 133, 134, 136, 137,
145, 146, 149, 150, 154, 155, 164—166, 180, 181, 184, 189
Märkisches Museum, Berlin: Vorsatz, 5, 13, 21, 22, 29—33, 37,
39, 41, 48, 63—65, 68, 71, 82, 107, 118, 131, 171, 172
»Der Morgen«, Berlin: 159
Service Photographique du Musée de Versailles, Paris: 19
Fotobestand Wolfgang Schäche, Berlin: 112
Sammlung Georg Schäfer, Schweinfurt: 34, 35
Axel Springer Privatbesitz, Berlin: 62
Staatliche Schlösser und Gärten, Berlin: 4, 15
Plansammlung der Technischen Universität Berlin: 3
Ullstein Bilderdienst, Berlin: 18, 24, 25, 28, 38, 42—44, 50,
52—59, 66, 67, 69, 70, 72—79, 84, 86—90, 92—95, 97—99, 102—106,
109, 113—116, 121, 123—125, 127, 128, 130, 132, 135, 138—144, 147,
148, 151—153, 156—158, 160—163, 167—169, 173—179, 182, 183, 187,
188, 190, 192—199, 201—207 sowie die Aufnahmen auf S. 37, 38
Ullstein Verlagsarchiv, Berlin: 12, 17, 23, 47, 49, 51, 60, 91, 108,
110, 111
Zenit Bildagentur, Berlin: 208

Die Abbildung auf dem Vorsatz zeigt das Panorama Berlins
um 1850, Lithographie von W. Loeillot. The fly-leaf shows
a panoramic view on Berlin around 1850, Lithography
by W. Loeillet.